Ho Chi Minh City: Top 10 Guide to

Copyright © 2012 by Green Talent Limited

Cover design by Green Talent Limited
Book design by Green Talent Limited

All rights reserved.

No part of this book may be reproduced in any form or by any electronic or mechanical means including information storage and retrieval systems, without permission in writing from the author. The only exception is by a reviewer, who may quote short excerpts in a review.

Green Talent Ltd
Visit my website at www.greentalent.co.uk

Printed in the United States of America

First Printing: 2012

ISBN: 978-1-291-20047-8

18,748 Words

235 Pages

184 Pictures

140 Reviews

Contents

Contents

Contents 4
About the Author 5
Introduction 6
What is not covered 8
Top 10 Hotels 9
Top 10 Restaurants 20
What to visit top 10 38
Top 10 Shopping 50
What to avoid top 10 63
Top 10 Night life 75
Top 10 Outside HCMC 86
Top 10 What to buy 125
Top 10 places to drink 136
Top 10 what to bring 146
Top 10 Language 157
Practical Information Top 10 159
Top 10 mixing with the locals 179
Understanding Vietnam Top 10 198
Top 10 pictures... or so 221
Other publications from Green Talent 229

About the Author

Tony Houseworth was born in London but grew up in Spain.

Author of four other books, currently works as journalist for The Guide of Vietnam, the best selling and biggest lifestyle magazine in Vietnam.

Crazy about traveling, fine wines and good food, he has travelled to over 25 countries, and lived in several.

He currently lives in Ho Chi Minh City and he has published a book on Vietnamese cultural differences aimed to expats, businessmen and travellers alike.

Introduction

Thanks for buying my guide to Ho Chi Minh City. I hope it will help you to have an even more memorable visit to this wonderful city and country.

Although I initially arrived as a tourist to Vietnam, I was enchanted by its magic, and decided to quit my job in London and move here, and since I have done nothing but enjoy the gratitude and kindness of its people.

When I visited as a tourist I brought three tourist guides, none of which really satisfied me, so I decided to write this one. If you are a similar traveller to me, I am sure you will enjoy the lack of clutter to fill pages, writing about what is important, and lots of tips that usually only locals know about.

This book will bring you to most interesting parts of Ho Chi Minh City, as well as to other parts of the country. Do not worry if you think I am not covering everything and you will be short of things to do and see: if you visit everything I review in this book, you will need three to four weeks!

I HOPE YOU ENJOY IT!

CHINA
Sapa
Babe
Lang Son
Dien Bien Phu
HANOI
Halong Bay
Hoa Lu
GULF OF TONKIN
Vinh
LAOS
Hue
Danang
Hoian
CAMBODIA
Buon Me Thuat
Nha Trang
Dalat
Tay Ninh
HO CHI MINH
Muine
Phu Quoc
My Tho
Can Tho
SOUTH CHINA SEA
GULF OF THAILAND

What is not covered

Something I do not like about many tourist guides, and where I want to make a difference, is the large amount of unnecessary, irrelevant information that just wastes readers' time and increases the weight of the book.

Unless you are planning to be here for 2-3 months you will have limited time, therefore I am giving you information of the best, not the most expensive, not the cheapest, simply the best.

Therefore in this guide you will not find anything about the number of rooms the hotels have, I am assuming that unless you are organising a wedding, you want one or two.

Phone numbers change often and new ones are available from the internet.

You do not get a long list of hotels or restaurants, but only what in my opinion are the best either for quality, value for money or both.

Even if you plan to spend two weeks in HCMC, this guide cover enough top attractions to keep you busy, so you will not find references to small pagodas or churches, small uninteresting markets, etc.

This guide is for the wise traveller who wants the best!

Top 10 Hotels

1.- Caravelle Hotel

19-23 Lam Son Square, D1

This is probably the best hotel in HCMC. If you like independently run hotels, offering amazing customer services and all the facilities you need, Caravelle Hotel is for you.

Situated in the heart of Saigon, it is walking distance from the Opera House, the Post Office, the Town Hall and many other of the top attractions.

With several bars and restaurants, the roof top bar offers the joy of latin music from a Cuban band. Two more reasons not to miss the roof top bar are the incredibly well prepared cocktails and the city views.

2.- Sheraton Hotel

Dong Khoi, D1

Sheraton hotel is located in the centre of Saigon, not far from the many tourist attractions like Notre Dame Cathedral, the Post Office and the Opera House.

Set in a side road to one of the most famous shopping streets in Saigon, it offers the usual high quality standards typical of the Sheraton Hotel chain.

The rooftop bar offers live music, incredible city views and a good selection of cocktails and other beverages.

3.- Park Hyatt Hotel

2 Lam Son Square, D1

Opposite Caravelle hotel, Park Hyatt has probably the most beautiful entrance of all the top hotels in Ho Chi Minh City: on arrival you can not miss the beautiful garden with numerous palm trees, making you feel like being somewhere else rather than in the very centre of Saigon.

Park Hyatt offers five star accommodation, and has a lovely piano bar with a great selection of wines.

4.- Intercontinental Hotel

Corner Hai Ba Trung and Le Duan, D1

Asiana Intercontinental Hotel s shares the location with Kumho Link, a restaurant and shopping mall with around 10 top international restaurants.

Located in the middle of District one, and walking distance from Notre Dame cathedral and other key touristic spots, Intercontinental offers many good dining options on its own restaurants as well as those available in Kumho Link, including Hard Rock café.

5.- Starcity Hotel

144 Nguyen Van Troi, Phu Nhuan

Starcity Hotel is a four star hotel located in the main road that takes from the airport to the city centre.

If you want to be closer to the airport, or simply you do not want to be located in the noisy but bubbly district one, Starcity hotel offers amazing accommodation at a very reasonable price.

Great buffet breakfast as well as bar with live music and a great selection of wines. Do not miss the cake corner!

Although not in the city centre, is just around 15 minutes away ($5 taxi drive) from district one.

6.- Blue Diamond Hotel

48 Thu Khoa Huan, D1

Blue Diamond is my favourite hotel in HCMC if you are looking for good value for money: this three star hotel with four star accommodation and service is located in the very heart of Saigon.

Five minutes walking from Ben Thanh Market and closely located for other tourist attractions, Blue Diamond Hotel offers great location, quality accommodation at bargain price.

Tip: the breakfast buffet is great.

7.-Renaissance Riverside Hotel

8-15 Ton Duc Thang, D1

Located by the river, and offering fantastic views, Renaissance hotel is a another addition to the five star hotel scene in Ho Chi Minh City.

Great service and location, one of the highlights of this hotel is the restaurant located in the ground floor: every night it offers a buffet dinner at reasonable price but huge quality: an amazing range of seafood, including lobster, sentinel crab, stone crab as well as sushi, sashimi and a great cheese bar and amazing dessert selection.

8.- Hotel Nikko Saigon

235 Nguyen Van Cuu, D1

Hotel Nikko is a new addition to the five star hotel Saigon scene.

Conveniently located in district one, this hotel is very well known for its food services.

With several restaurants and new food promotions every month, Nikko hotel is well known amongst the locals as a great place for excellent food and service.

9.- Hotel Rex

141 Nguyen Hue, D1

Rex hotel is yet another five star hotel situated in district one, the heart of Saigon.

Within walking distance of the local amenities, one of the highlights of this luxury hotel is the restaurant in the roof top serving top quality Vietnamese food.

The views on the restaurant are great and so is the service.

10.- New World Hotel

76 Le Lai, D1

Situated walking distance of Benh Thanh market, New World hotel is another five star hotel offering top quality accommodation in Ho Chi Minh City.

Virtually opposite one of the main parks of Saigon, the views are very nice, and just a walk apart of most attractions.

Top 10 Restaurants

1.- Renaissance Hotel Restaurant

8-15 Ton Duc Thang, D1

My girlfriend surprised me by booking a table at this restaurant, no particular reason, she just wanted us to enjoy the amazing seafood buffet they offer in the evenings.

The only problem you will face is to choose amongst the many possibilities on offer, and even if you are a big eater, as I am, expect not to be able to try even half of them.

With a lovely salad table, with several options to choose mixing both eastern and western choices, some green will make a good start.

Different types of sushi and sashimi, as well as soup, cold meats, rice and pasta, will give you plenty to try for starters.

The highlight is fresh seafood and fish, once you reach the counter you can choose from lobster, different types of crab and fish as well as king prawns and clams.

The toughest decision was to choose between the cheese board and the different home made desserts, all of them delicious.

2.- The Deck.

38 Nguyen U DI, Thao Dien, An Phu, D 2

If you are looking for something really special without having to break the bank, you should visit The Deck in District 2.

The Deck gives you the chance to try fantastic fusion food, while looking at the tranquillity of the river within a modern and stylish environment.

The garden is fantastic, and so is the service from arrival at The Deck. Tables overlooking the river are just brilliant but food is amazing: we tried Nha Trang oysters with 3 different sauces (200.000 vnd) as well beef Carpaccio (230.000 vnd) both of them had a great presentation and even greater taste. However the star of the meal was the seabass (280.000 vnd) served with a pesto sauce, it is just the best seabass I have ever had.

The Deck offers a complete wine list and an extensive cocktail menu, with a huge variety of martinis which go half price at happy hour from 4 to 7.

If apart from great food and an amazing experience you are after exclusivity, The Deck has recently started offering boat taxi pick up from district one, as well as a selection of lunch and sunset cruises, where you will have the boat and service just for your party.

Open 7 days a week, whether you want to have amazing food or just to chill out having some drinks, the Deck is the place.

3.- Le Caprice

The Landmark, Ton Duc Thang, D1

Le Caprice is located on the top of the Landmark building next to the river in District 1.

It is one of the finest restaurants, offering amazingly well prepared and presented French food.

Although the prices are not cheap, it is highly recommended for a special occasion: the food is marvellous and so is the service you receive and the views, especially at night.

Le Caprice also offers a reasonable priced extensive wine list, great companion for such a gourmet experience.

4.- Kitahama

Mac Din Chi, D1

I love Japanese food as much as I love variety, however this restaurant hidden in District one must have something really special as every time I am out for Japanese food I end up there.

With an extensive menu, some of the highlights of this little restaurant are the sushi and sashimi options, all very fresh and delicious.

Different sakes as well as bottled beers and tap are available and expect to be surrounded by Japanese customers, expats and tourists alike who seem to know how good this hidden jewel is.

5.- New York Steak House

25 Nguyen Dinh Chieu, D1

Close to the zoo you can find New York Steakhouse. If apart from good service, you love good quality well and prepared steaks, this is the place to visit in Saigon, no doubt!

The layout and the decoration takes you to a classic steakhouse in the US, with well presented black and white pictures of celebrities on the walls, awhile Chaplin's movies play in the background. The moment you arrive to your table, you know that every detail has and will be taken care of.

The core of the menu is angus beef imported directly from the US. Different cuts are offered, and you can choose between beef from Chicago and organically grown beef from California. A well designed drink list is available, with a good selection of wines by the glass, as well as cocktails and other beverages.

With a glass of St Emilion Cheval Noir we started with the Beef Carpaccio, which was lovely presented; the mix of rocket salad, thinly sliced raw beef, parmesan cheese and thick balsamic vinegar brought an explosion of well combined flavours to the mouth, a great sensation for a mere 180.000VND.

Beef steaks start at 440.000VND for a 250gr sirloin steak, but sizes available go up to 800gr, if this is not enough, you can choose the weigh too. Before steaks are served, the waiter will bring you a knife box, for you to choose your favourite knife to cut your steak, a ceremony that will surely impress your guests.

Around 18 side dishes are available, ranging from 50.000 to 95.000VND; I strongly recommend the creamy truffles spinach and sauted corn and bacon, as both are amazing.

We tried the sirloin steak and the rib eye which arrived with three different sauces as well as a selection of flavoured salts and four different types of mustard; very well presented but the best is the taste, which is difficult to be found in Vietnam, just amazing, we were in paradise!

If you like good quality beef and a great dining experience, you must visit New York Steakhouse.

6.- 98

98 Hoa Phuong, Phu Nhuan

Please tell no one, this restaurant, walking distance from my home, is my big secret!

Hidden in a little road in Phu Nhuan district, restaurant 98 offers an amazing selection of fresh seafood and fish; and it could not be fresher as they keep everything alive!

Prices are very low as they cater for the locals, however expect to be seated in a plastic chair and be served in an aluminium table.

Kitchen is open air so you can judge by yourself about the cleanliness and cooking style, but you will not regret visiting this place if you love seafood, don't leave without trying sentinel crab and giant mussels!

7.- Pacharan

95 Hai Ba Trung, D1

Located in the heart of district 1, walking distance from the Opera house and other amenities, Pacharan is the top Spanish restaurant in Saigon.

Whether you want to go for some tapas or a la carte menu, you will not be disappointed. Nor will you with the amazing Spanish wine list, cocktails and offering one of the best served beers on tap in Saigon.

Wednesdays, Fridays and Saturdays are even more interesting due to live music on the first floor, offering an incredible environment, great music and drinks.

8.- Jaspas

33 Dong Khoi, D1, and 74/7 Hai Ba Trung, D1,

Part of Alfresco's group, Jaspas offers a wide range of international food, combining Asian and Western flavours.

Jaspas has recently launched a new lunch set menu at its Dong Khoi eatery; weekdays from 11.30 to 14.30 you can enjoy a fantastic three course meal for just 200.000VND. For the starter you will be invited to the salad buffet that includes five freshly made salads which change daily, plus you have the possibility of making your own as a large variety of ingredients and dressings are available as well as a mixing bowl. You can also try the soup the day, as well as several cold meats.

With such variety of salads I had to try them all, and I must say that the butter beans and tomato, and farfalle salads were my favourites.

For main course I chose the grilled tender beef medallion served with wasabi mash, greens and red wine gravy. It was absolutely delicious; I was also tempted by the other four main courses, especially the Asian seabass in tomato and herb sauce.

Part of the set menu, the dessert buffet offers five different rich desserts plus fresh fruit. I tried the apple strudel, the cheesecake and the rice pudding, all of them amazing.

The a la carte menu is huge, including 9 types of stake alone.

Apart from the quality and variety, I was seriously impressed by the freshness of the ingredients and the amazing customer service.

9.- Good Morning Vietnam

197 De Tham St. District 1

With three restaurants in Vietnam, Good Morning Vietnam has spent the last 14 years pleasing Italian food lovers.

The first restaurant opened in HCMC in 1998, you can find it at 198 De Tham street, virtually opposite Sinh Café bus operator. Open daily from 9am to 12pm, Good Morning Vietnam brings you authentic Italian taste as well as Italian hospitality. The secret for its success is that apart from using virtually all original Italian ingredients (the main exception is beef which is brought from New Zealand), the head chef is Italian and they do care a lot for providing highest standards both in quality and service. He daily checks the quality and storage of food, making sure that the standards are very high.

When we visited the Saigon branch of Good Morning Vietnam we tried a new dish, the Carpaccio di Pesce, made out of three different types of raw fish with a very delicate lemon based marinade. I can say it was just absolutely fantastic, so delicious that I need to have it again very soon.

Hesitating whether to have pasta or pizza as main course, we finally decided to try both. We started with the delicious Penne alla vodka, what could I say, fantastic! With a rich cream based sauce, this pasta dish was amazing, very big portion and for just 130.000 VND is a steal!

The key success for the pizza pepperoni, which we tried next, is not only the quality of the pepperoni (Italian spicy sausage), but the quality and quantity of the cheese used on it, plus the dole being 100% hand made. It was very nice but we could not finish it, as we really wanted to try one of the homemade desserts.

Time for pannacota al cioccolato. Presentation was great, and the taste was just fantastic. Again generous portion was served and just for 70.000 VND.

Wondering how the food would differ I decided to also visit Good Morning Vietnam in Mui Ne. Situated in the main road opposite Bamboo Village Resort, the Mui

Ne branch of Good Morning Vietnam offers both outdoors and indoors seating. Also under Italian management, and with the same commitment to food quality and great service, we were pleased to try some different dishes.

The Carpaccio di Manzo (Beef carpaccio) at 110.000 VND was very delicious and served in an unusual huge portion. Hesitating again between pizza and pasta, we had to try both! We chose the Pizza Crudo e Parmigiano for 125.000 VND, which was prepared in a wood fired oven, following a design from Naples. It was very nice and tasty.

For pasta we were presented with Gnocchi al Pesto 105.000 VND, the pasta, which is home made, was again absolutely delicious, so delicate that it melts in your mouth. Not only the price is rather low considering the quality of the ingredients, but the portions are quite big.

Another of the secrets of Good Morning Vietnam is that its staff has been in the company for 10 years, so they know how to do the job pretty well. This can also be experienced if you try the delicious coffee in either of the restaurants. If you are a espresso lover, or simply like good coffee, you can't leave without trying it here.

Great delicious food from high quality ingredients, great customer service, and a passion for Italian food explains the success of this company, with around 95% of customers returning on a regular basis.

10.- Au Parc

23 Han Thuyen, D1

Located in the heart of District 1, just a few minutes away from the Cathedral and the Unification Palace, Auparc offers an amazing combination of middle eastern and Mediterranean flavours.

With several floors and seating options to choose from, whether you come for coffee or for a full meal, you will not be disappointed at Auparc.

The menu is really extensive with lots of appealing choices. We decided to start with the fresh salmon and smoked seabass carpaccio (110.000 vnd), which was served with a garlic and lemon sauce; very well presented and great flavours.

For main course we decided to try two different kebabs: both the beef kebab and the shish kebab (lamb) shared the garlic, cumin and ginger marinade, which was delicious. Both were served with a large portion of chips, salad and a metze, more than enough to fill the most hungry.

If you are looking for a good meal, in good environment at relatively low prices, you should visit Auparc, what is more, Mr Loi and his crew will make sure that you will have a great experience on top of delicious food.

What to visit top 10

1.- Notre Dame cathedral

Ben Nghe, D1

This smaller replica of the French historic cathedral is a must visit.

Situated in the centre of district one, dominates the main city (Paris)square, walking distance from the post office and unification palace, is very nice on its own, plus if you are lucky you may enjoy he ceremony and photo taking of one of the many local weddings.

Part of the French colonial heritage, is one of the must see in Saigon.

2.- Post Office

Ben Nghe, D1

Also part of the French colonial heritage, the post office building, which is still in use, is one of the most beautiful buildings in Saigon.

Located in Paris square, in district one, is walking distance from Notre Dame Cathedral, and a few more amenities.

Try to avoid the many postcard, stamps and virtually anything sellers by its door, as they truly overcharge for everything as they are aware of this being one of the top touristic spots. Most sale items can be purchased at a much reduced price inside the post office.

3.- Opera House

Dong Khoi, D1

In the intersection of Le Loi and Dong Khoi you can find the opera house buildings, one of the most beautiful buildings in HCMC.

Inspired by nearby buildings belonging to the old French quarter, the Opera House is a must see, not to mention that usually for a low price you can enjoy one of the many high quality performances.

4.- City Hall

Le Thanh Ton, D1

Its construction started in the late 19th century and was inaugurated in early 20th century. It has a lovely bell tower.

Now in between shopping centres, this architectural piece remains one of the main government buildings, so police will stop you from taking photos next to it, however you are usually allowed to take them from the park opposite it,

5.- Reunification Palace

Nam Ky Khoi Nghia

Walking distance from Notre Dame Cathedral you can find the Reunification Palace, surrounded by huge gardens.

It used to be known as Independence Palace, used to be the workplace of the President of South Vietnam during the war.

Although there is nothing special about the building, the surroundings are great, and so is the history contained inside; do not miss the underground passages to the kitchen and the emergency communications room, really worth a visit.

Beautiful views from the open roof, especially if you are looking for good photos.

6.- War Remnants Museum

28 Vo Van Tan, D3

It mostly contains exhibits related to the American invasion during the Vietnam war.

Located in what it used to the premises of the US Information Agency, until very recently used to be called the Exhibition House of US Crimes, and only recently changed its name.

One of the most popular museums in Vietnam, if you have the time it is really worth visiting.

7.- Golden dragon Water Puppet Theatre

55B Nguyen Thi Minh Khai, D1

Probably a heritage from the Chinese influence, the Water Puppet show is a must. Located next to Tao Dan park.

If you are looking for an unusual but beautiful performance, this is a must see for children and adults alike. Don't worry about the language, just enjoy the show.

Tip: book in advance, as the theatre is small and sells out very quickly.

8.- Dam Sen Water Park

3 Hoa Binh, D11

This is an amusement park in the outskirts of HCMC, very popular with the locals, looking to have a different day out.

Although it is water themed, offering water slides of all sorts, you can also find other activities.

Entry fee is rather low (around $5 for the day), and you are ensured to have fun, without having to suffer the long queues of similar attractions in the west.

9.- Vietnam History Museum

2 Nguyen Binh Khiem, D1

This museum shows a large amount of items and artefacts from Vietnamese history as well as many historical treasures.

Many interesting items, and one of the few museums in Vietnam with English explanations.

The museum is hosted in a rather nice abuilding which is also worth a look.

10.- Suoi Tien Theme Park

120 AH1,Tan Phu, D9

Located around 15 km away from Ho Chi Minh City, this theme park is the first park in the world dedicated to Buddhism.

The museum has chosen many of the sacred animals to be represented in the park, also focusing in Vietnamese history and folklore.

Another attraction of the park is the crocodile world holding well over 1.000 live crocodiles which can be fed!

Top 10 Shopping

1.- Ben Thanh Market

Le Loi, D1

Ben Thanh Market is tourist paradise for shopping, or maybe the other way round! Situated in district 1 and open until around 5pm every day, BTM offers absolutely everything you want to buy from fresh flowers and alive fish to clothes, souvenirs and electronics.

Containing hundreds of stalls, expect to be asked to buy from each of them by the keen sales attendants.

Although some locals buy here, it is mostly aimed to tourists (foreigners and Vietnamese alike), and expect to bargain hard in order to get a fair price.

Once the market closes, may of the stalls will move their merchandise outside and set it up around the market building ready for the night market.

No aircon, so be prepared!

Tip: try one of the restaurant stalls in the middle of the market, delicious and affordable seafood fresh from the fish stalls!

2.- Saigon Square

7 Ton Duc Thanh, D1

Saigon square is a very popular shopping gallery, set over three floors, walking distance from Ben Thanh Market.

You will mostly find clothes and accessories here but also some electronics, fake dvds and bags.

Although you can try bargaining, you will not need to do so as hard as in Ben Thanh market, as most stalls offer fixed price.

Very popular with the locals, very good for clothing and for finding bargains.

Tip: you can relax in the recently opened luxury Fresco Café, next to Saigon Square, offering one of the best coffees in Saigon.

3.- The Tax Department

135 Nguyen Hue, D1

The tax department offers a mix of well known brands (perfume, electronics), in the ground floor, with clothing, shoes, bags and souvenirs in the remaining floors.

Everything here, or most of it, is fixed price, so don't expect to have to bargain.

Different quality standards, especially on the upper floors, with many fakes at "bargain" prices around… watch out for very expensive low quality Chinese fakes of brand shoes!

4.- Vincom Center

75 Le Thanh Ton, D1

Vin Con center is luxury shoppers paradise. Imitating many of the popular high end shopping centers in the West, Vin Con has recently opened its second building next to original one.

Here you will find the most popular international brands, as well as a large amount of fast food restaurants and a gaming area.

Very popular with Vietnamese and foreigners alike, you easily spend a full day here window shopping

5.- Diamond Plaza

34 Le Duan, D1

Diamond Plaza is hosted in a new beautiful building opposite Notre Dame Cathedral.

With top brands selling authentic goods over three floors, it also hosts a small gourmet supermarket as well as a cinema in the top floor and bowling and entertainment arena.

The dining area, hosting mostly fast food outlets, has recently been renovated and expanded and it is very popular with shoppers and teenagers, as prices are quite reasonable.

6.- Parksons

45 Le Thanh Ton, D1

Parksons was one of the first companies to open luxury department stores in HCMC, with one of its flag stores opposite Vincom centre.

Although with different style, it offers very similar brands to Vincom, and a recent addition is an outlet of the Body Shop.

Many luxury brands, and very spacious peaceful environment, ideal for a rest if you want to kill some time before visiting the Opera house.

7.- Cho Tan Dinh

48 Ma Lo, D1

This local market in the border of districts one and Phu Nhuan, used to cater just for the locals, however with its proximity to a very nice church and district one is starting to receive the invasion of tourists, and may become the Ben Thanh market of the north soon.

Usual mix of everything, good to get fresh flowers.

Tip: be very careful with the traffic outside, terribly dangerous!

8.- Cho Ba Chieu

Bach Dang, Binh Thanh

This market in Benh Thanh district is one of the most authentic local markets, hardly any foreigners visit it so be expected to be pointed at and become the attraction of the locals.

On the inside you can find a mix of clothing, kitchenware and virtually everything.

Around the market on the outside, lots of stalls selling fruit, worth a look for unusual tropical fruits, meat, fish and a few eating places.

If you are out for the unusual look for the stalls selling frogs, which on sale will weight them, and them cut the legs and head to then skin them alive…

And if you are adventurous enough, try the food in one of the many food stalls, all very cheap!

9.- Vincom 2

116 Nguyen Hue, D1

Also known as Vincom A or new Vincom, this new super department store opened its doors in October 2012.

Walking distance from its predecessor, and still with many outlets to be opened, this commercial center brings more and new luxury shops to the centre of Saigon.

It also has a good selection of restaurants and coffee shops, but watch out for the "speciality" coffee being sold by Trung Nguyen at premium prices: it is mixed with corn!

10.- Parkson Tan Son Nhat

60 A Truong Son, Tanbinh

Located virtually opposite the airport, this new Parksons store give shoppers the opportunity to do last minute shopping before taking their flight back home.

Laid over different floors there are lots of shops representing international brands; from cosmetics to shoes and clothes, without forgetting hand bags, this is paradise for shoppers.

What to avoid top 10

1.- Hai Long Hotels

59 Hai Ba Trung, D1

Having visited over 25 countries, this hotel chain is the worst I have ever experienced, in particular Hailong 5 in Hai Ba Trung.

This chain represents everything what Vietnam should get rid of: overpriced, miss sold description of rooms, bellboys going the extra mile to get any business out of you, including prostitution, rooms with no water, or hot water only,...

Rooms advertised with window, for which you pay extra do usually have a window...looking at the hall... beds full of bugs, noisy,... great long list of things you don't want.

2.- Fake taxis

Vietnam has many taxi companies, however many of them are fake, i.e., you get your car, put some stickers on it, and hey you are a taxi driver ready to overcharge tourist.

Some of the "legal" taxis are aware and even promote their drivers to cheat the meters and every now and then the meter will simply jump.

Tip: if you want to be safe, use Vinataxi or Mailinh, there are plenty of them, and usually they are great.

3.- Fake coffee

Not long ago, I published an article about this on the national press: in case you did not know, Vietnam is the largest producer of coffee in the world; you can get lots of types and very cheap, however in many coffee shops they will buy cheaper versions which are mixed with corn, green beans and all sorts of chemicals, coffee simply tastes weird, and although it is unlikely to make you ill, it is not ideal, especially when you are paying premium prices!

The tradition of this mix, started after the war, difficult times, and anything was to be done to make ends meet, unfortunately nowadays some rogue companies continue the practice.

Tip: for good coffee, try one of the many coffee shops of Fresco Café, Highlands or Coffee Bean and if you want to buy to bring home visit Anam market in Hai Ba Trung.

4.- Traffic

Is not so much about traffic jams, but much more about getting closer to traffic: Vietnamese can't simply don't drive, and probably don't know that motorbikes have breaks (or actually refuse to use them).

Seriously traffic is a real danger even (especially) if you are a pedestrian, as they respect no rules.

Expect motorbikes to come into the pavement, especially on peak hours, and they will expect you to move out

5.-Fake alcohol

Fake alcohol, especially spirits is very common in Vietnam, and apart from the likely terrible hangover there are also some health dangers involved.

Chivas and Johnnie Walker are two of the most copied spirits as they are very popular, try to buy in big international shops, which tend to make an effort to ensure the quality of their products.

Although buying in supermarkets is relatively safe, not always…definitely do not buy in markets!

6.- Scams

This applies to everyone, but to men in particular: if you are traveling solo and you get approached by some woman or women pretending to be tourists and engaging on friendly conversation be very aware!

Although I did not get scammed, on three occasions they tried, and I must said they were very convincing, probably because they were nor young nor good looking, there was not sex involved and they were very convincing with their stories…in one of the cases I had to run away!

In all occasions the scammers were not Vietnamese but Asian, speaking very good English, they pretended to be Thai but my guess is that they were from Philippines.

7.- Drugs

Drugs in Vietnam are illegal, ok same as in most countries, the difference is that Vietnamese Government is very keen in keeping Vietnam as much as a drug free country as possible, and death penalty and long prison sentences do help to achieve so.

Once in district one, especially in the tourist quarter, drugs will be offered to you no doubt, you may even pay for them, however be aware of what you get: for what I have been told from many sources, you get anything but what you expect to buy.

Although you may be able to get some kind of heroin if you have the right contacts, you can forget about cocaine and hashish (taima). You may get something that looks and smells like it (remember this is the country that using chemicals can sell coffee from no coffee beans!) but definitely not what you want, and bringing high health risks!

8.- On the street seafood

You will find many appealing street eateries selling all sorts of seafood at very low prices, temptation is there, however watch out not only for the cleanliness of the place but especially for how the keep the food before cooking it!

In my experience, and remember in Vietnam temperatures are around 35 degrees, most of these street seafood restaurants keep the seafood at room temperature, and as they are set on the street: street temperature!

You just need one very bad experience, and my first one sent me to hospital, to be careful, but it is up to you to take the risk!

9.-Walking

I love walking and hiking, and I have tried many times walking in Vietnam, and although it is a possibility, it is a rather dangerous one:

First the pavement is usually in a rather bad estate with lots of broken paths, holes, cables and iron bars coming out of it.

However the main danger are motorbikes. My record is being hit twice in the same day while walking. Here the "culture" is for you to see and avoid the motorbikes even when you are walking on the pavement, this is especially the case during rush hour, where many motorbikes who can not wait the minute or so of a red light to turn green, will go on the pavement at full speed.

10.- Ice and straws outside main cities.

It may be common sense, however in most of the countryside and even some major cities like Hue, sellers of drinks, especially by main tourist attractions, will use unfiltered tap water for making ice for the drinks: although commercial ice is really inexpensive, people will go the extra mile to reduce costs.

The same applies to straws in drinks: I have seen a few times how the take the used straws and they throw them into a bucket of water to "clean" them and reuse them…

Top 10 Night life

1.- Seventeen Saloon

103A Pham Ngu Lao, D1

Saloon 17 is in the heart of backpackers area and offers the best live music in Saigon.

With two different floors offering different styles, it is themed in the far west, when I was taken there the first time, one of the things that caught my eye was waitresses' skirts being shorter than my underwear… but that apart music and atmosphere are great, food is fine and good selection of drinks.

The ground floor offers classic rock by an amazing band from Philippines, and top floor offers a mix of electronic, pop, disco,…

2.- Acoustic

6 E1 Ngo Thoi Nhiem, D3

Acoustic is one of the classic live music places in HCMC. Mostly visited by Vietnamese only, do not expect variety of drinks or nice decoration, however drinks are cheap, and you will enjoy several good live bands every night.

The atmosphere is great, and if you want to mingle with the locals, this is the place to go for live music.

3.- Saigon Saigon Bar

19-23 Lam Son Square, D1

Saigon Saigon Bar is in the top floor of Caravelle Hotel and everyday but Tuesdays offers live latin music, currently by Cuban band Corazon latino.

From salsa to merengue, but also bachata and cumbia, if you are into latin music, this is one of the best places to enjoy a good quality band.

With plenty of space to dance, you can also enjoy the fantastic cocktail list in a rather relaxed environment.

4.- Pacharan Live music

95 Hai Ba Trung, D1

Wednesday, Friday and Saturdays are the best days to enjoy live music in the first floor of Pacharan restaurant. Bands rotate, but the latin band Warapo guarantees to get the place very crowded: amazing music and a band that knows how to engage the public...also expect that at some points the singers will jump into the bar and sing and dance there.

Apart from the music, see review of the restaurant plus the also have a good selection of single malt whiskeys and cocktails

5.- Sheraton Level 23 Bar

Dong Khoi, D1

Usually frequented by famous locals, the roof bar in the Sheraton hotel offers live music most nights.

A mix of pop and rock is being played but the current band. The place is spacious and if you are lucky to get one of the tables, you will enjoy the comfy sofas.

Great drinks menu with very well prepared cocktails.

6.- Piano bar at Quo Vadis

5/7 Nguyen Sieu, D1

Quo Vadis, just off Hai Ba Trung (virtually opposite to Pacharan) is in a small hidden alley.

Don't be put off by the looks of the alley as once you close the door you will enter a world of luxury.

Great place for coffee, milkshakes and also for cocktails and wine, the best is the atmosphere, and most evening the live music from the pianist, ideal to relax or for a romantic occasion.

7.- Hard Rock Café

39 Le Duan, D1

Hard Rock Café is hosted as part of Kumho Link complex in District one, although they serve food, if it is not your cup of tea, you can pop into one of the many restaurants that the complex offers.

Hard Rock Café is huge, but it can get busy. Is one of the chosen place for birthdays and big parties, although one of the reasons I like it most is the rock live music taking place virtually every night

Try the different variety of mojitos!

8.- Napoly, top floor

7 Pham Ngoc Thach, D3

Although it is not its main business, Napoli is another of Saigon's hidden gems for live music, offering mix of pop and rock by a good band from Philippines.

Comfy seats, and a vast drinks and cocktails list, the main business of Napoli's first floor is being a gentlemen's club, so don't be scared by the very few female customers or by the many gorgeous female waitresses and hostesses.

This place is usually frequented by groups of men looking for a nice place, good music and the company of gorgeous women, which is also available straight away…just company, not prostitution: there are many gorgeous girls whose job is to join you in the table, give you good conversation and "help" you drink as much as possible.

9.- Bui Bar

39/2 Pham Ngoc Thac, D3

Bui is very similar to Napoli offering live music, with a mix of pop and rock by another good band from Philippines.

Comfy seats, and a vast drinks and cocktails list, the main business of Napoli's first floor is being a gentlemen's club, so don't be scared by the very few female customers or by the many gorgeous female waitresses and hostesses.

This place is usually frequented by groups of men looking for a nice place, good music and the company of gorgeous women, which is also available straight away…just company, not prostitution: there are many gorgeous girls whose job is to join you in the table, give you good conversation and "help" you drink as much as possible.

10.- Blanchy's Tash

95 Hai Ba Trung, D1

Blanchy's Tash opened not long ago, and seems to be a real success with foreigners and locals alike.

Split over three floors, it mixes a lounge with a restaurant and different international DJs playing hip music.

Also known as the Ibiza of Saigon, if you are after something new, this is the place to be.

Top 10 Outside HCMC

1.- Mekong delta

A visit to the Mekong Delta is a must if you are spending time in Saigon and you have an extra day.

There are several tourist companies who offer tours for around $30 dollars, picking you up from your hotel, taking you to see the delta, visit farms, factories and the jungle.

It is one of the best experiences of visiting Vietnam as it is rather unusual and unique.

Tip: carry mosquito repellent with you, and if you decide to walk out of the path of the tour be aware of the many snakes around, most of which will kill you; but as long as you stay with the group you will be safe as snakes run away from the noise.

2.- Vung Tau

Vung Tau is just under two hours away from Saigon by boat, and probably the closest sea spot with a decent beach.

It has a bad reputation, as being an oil city, sometimes you can smell the oil being pumped nearby if you get the wrong type of wind.

Having said that move to the new resorts where the beaches are totally unspoilt and clean to have a totally different experience.

Very good for seafood restaurants at affordable prices.

Tip: visit the natural park in the top of the hill via cable car; it is nice and views are amazing.

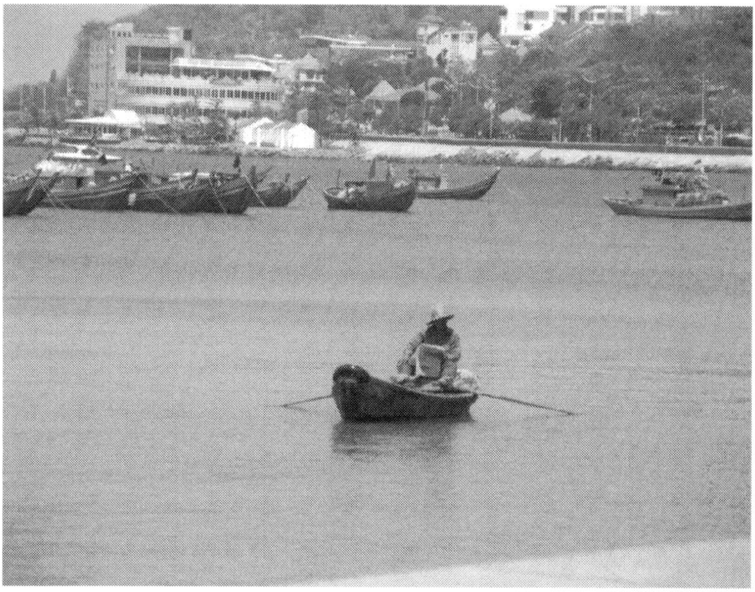

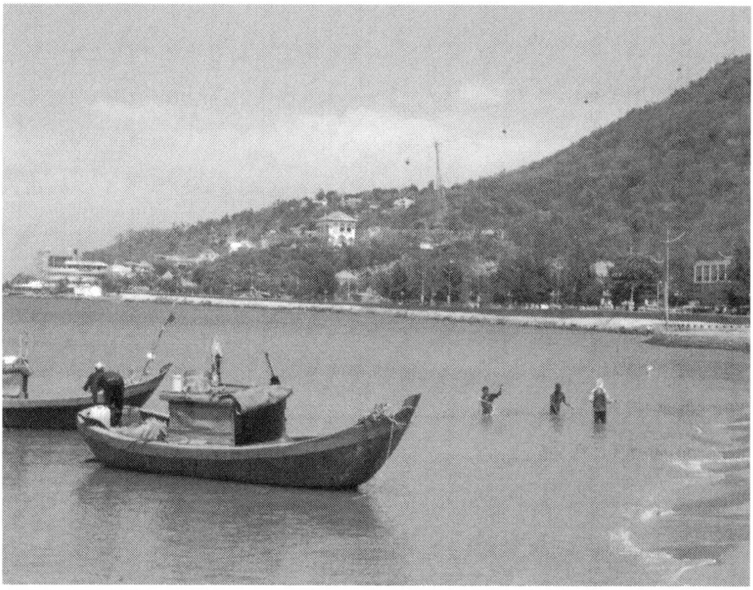

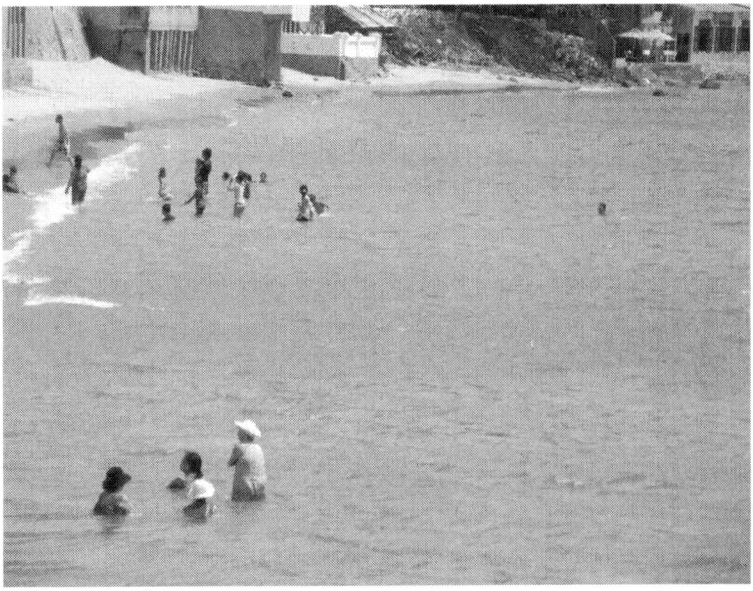

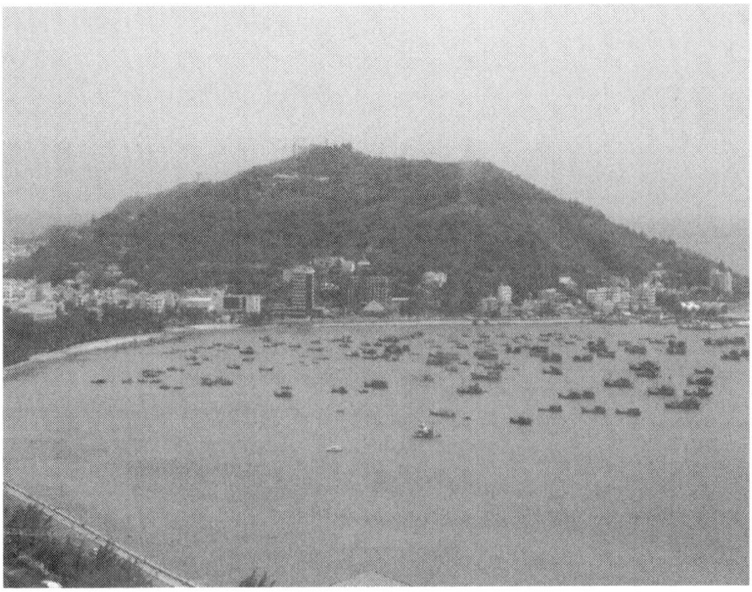

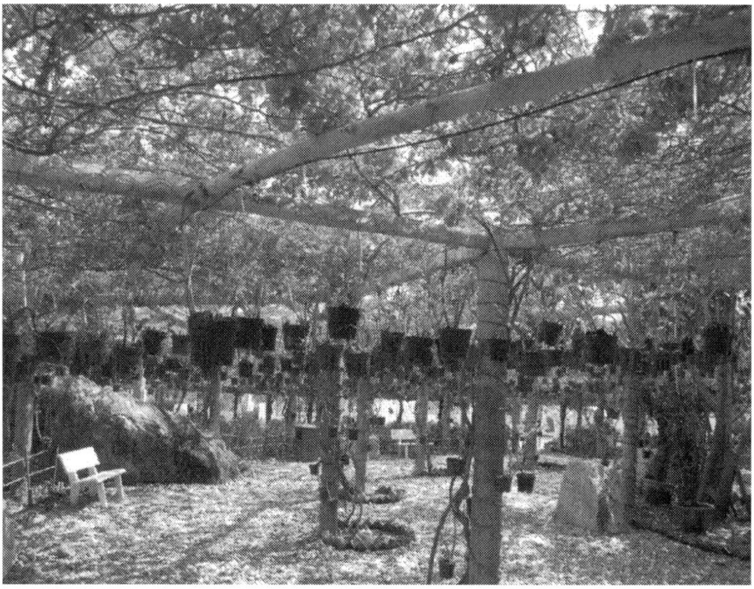

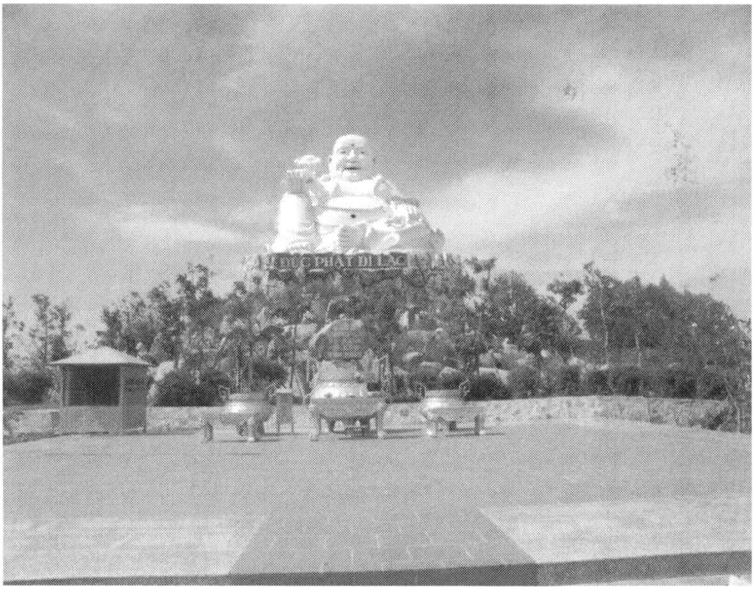

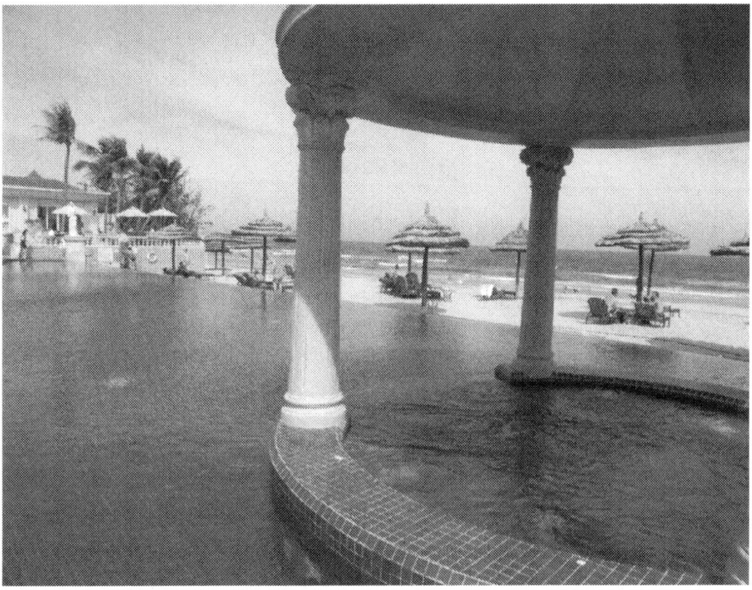

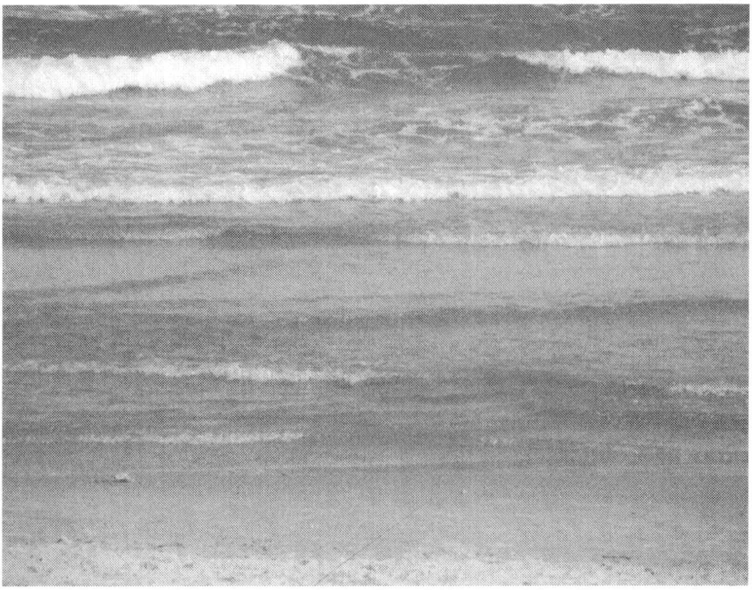

3.- Nha Trang

Nha Trang is the most developed coastal area, about one hour flight from HCMC.

Apart from the beautiful beach and seaside, the hospitality standards bust to what we westerners are used to. Very active night life too.

Tip try a cross islands day cruise, they are usually just $10 per person and a great experience.

Tip: do not mix Cyclo café, amazing service and food (try the ostrich)

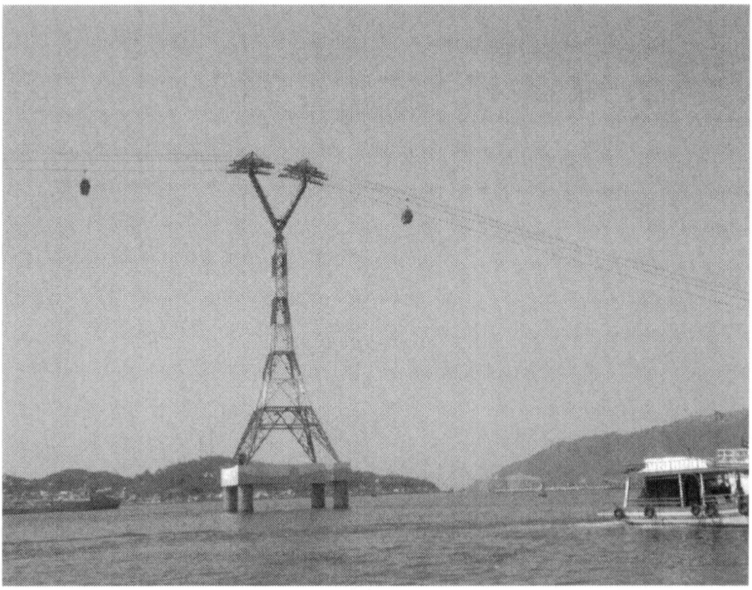

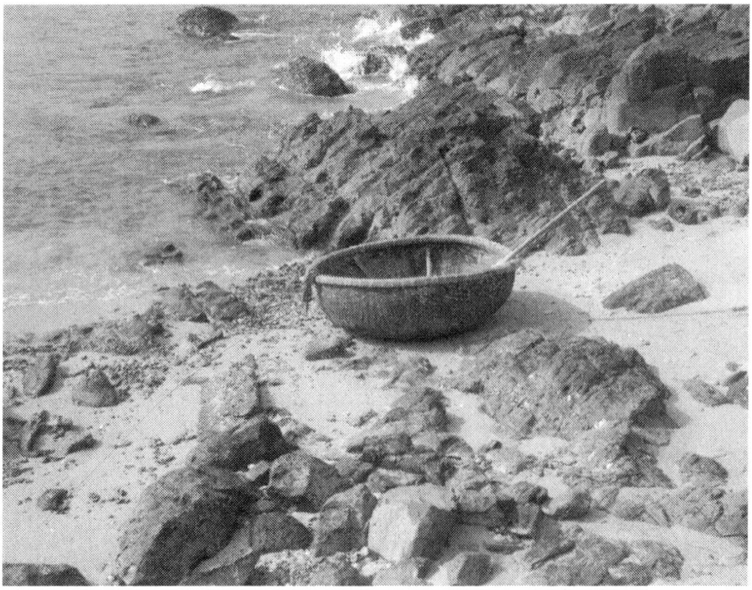

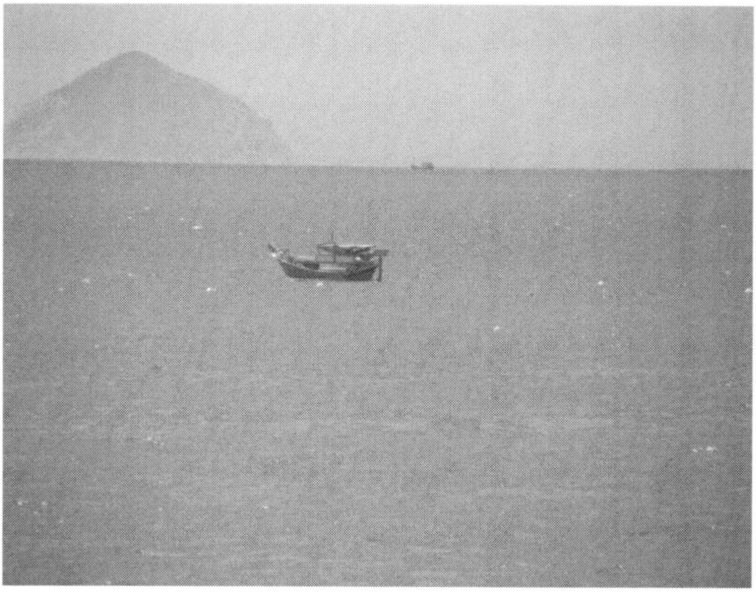

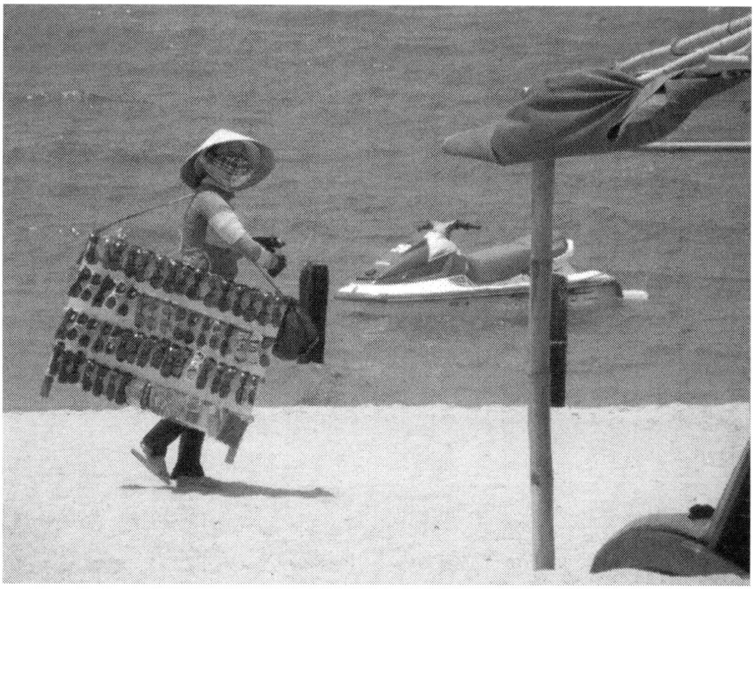

4.- Mui Ne

Mui Ne is somehow in between Nha Trang and HCMC, around 4-5 hours by coach will take you there, with many daily coaches available from HCMC.

Less developed than Nha Trang but with a huge developing potential, it mostly caters for Russian tourism, as you will see in the Cyrillic characters in the shops.

New developments have brought a decent amount of luxury resorts which will allow you to enjoy the fantastic seaside, Bamboo Village and Seahorse resorts are just paradise!

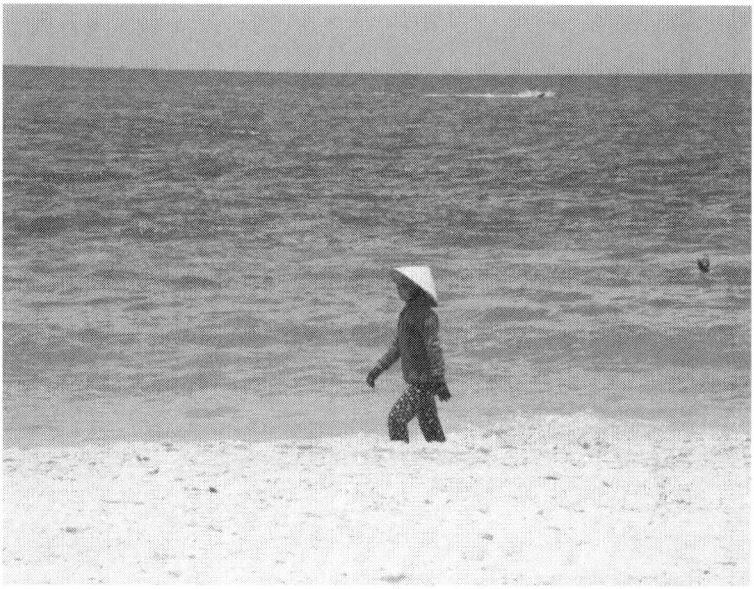

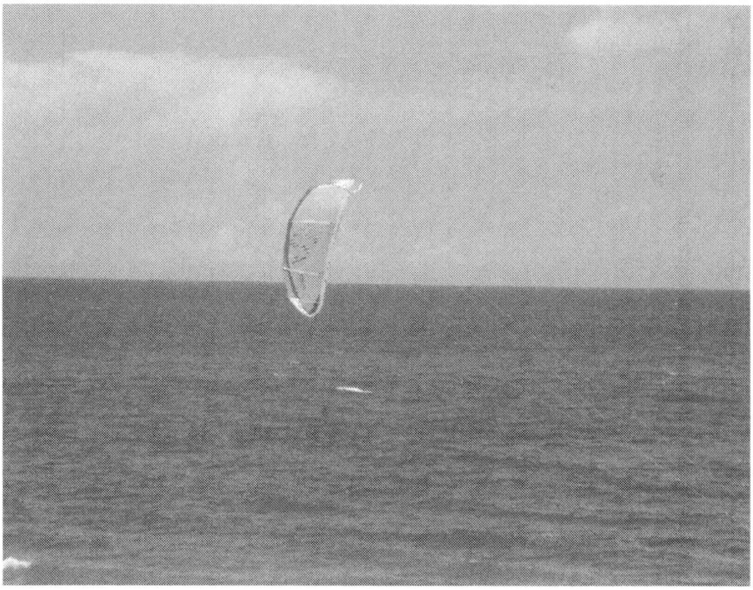

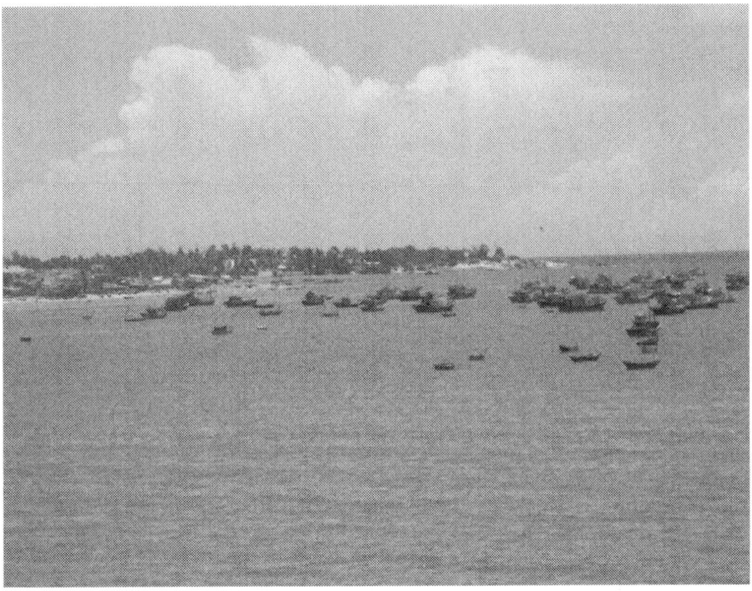

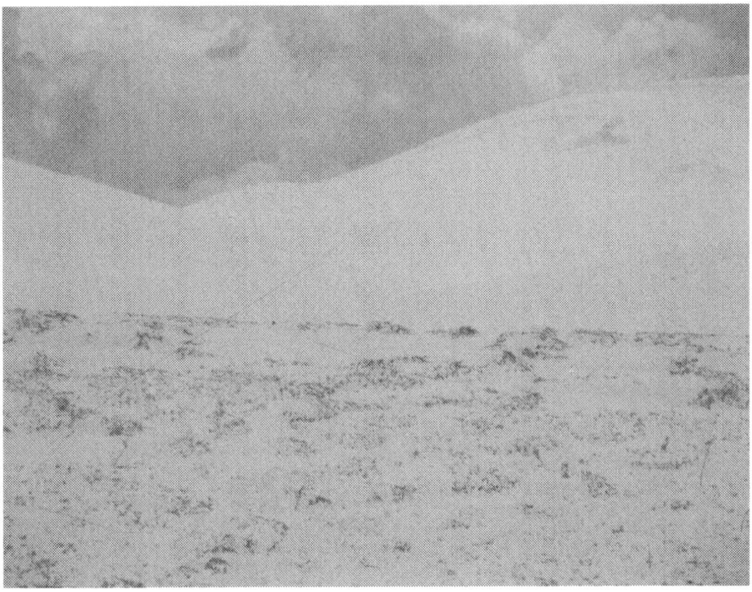

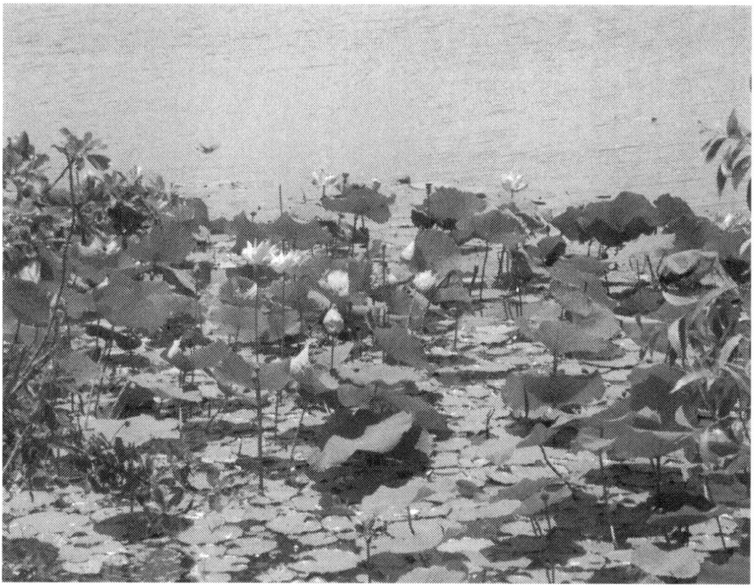

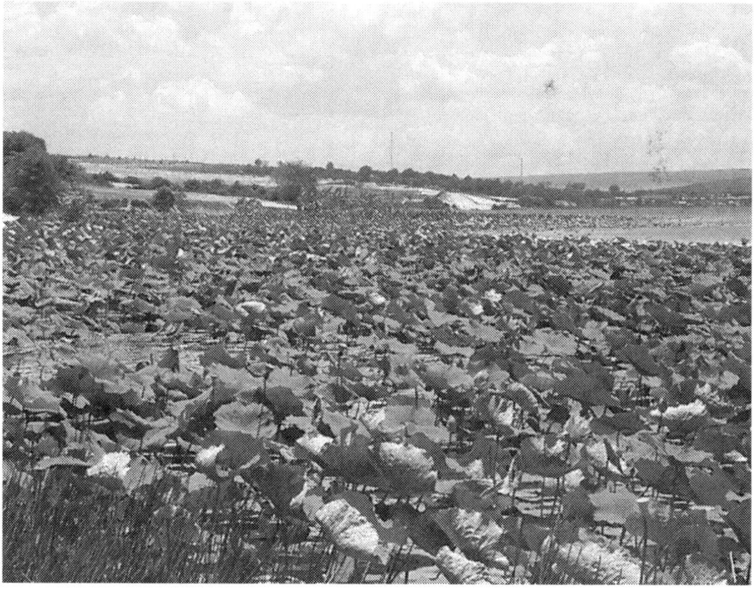

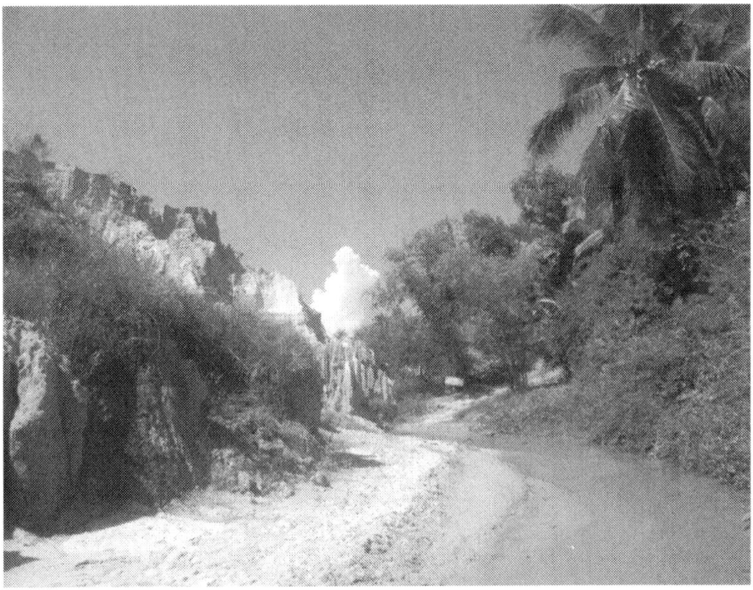

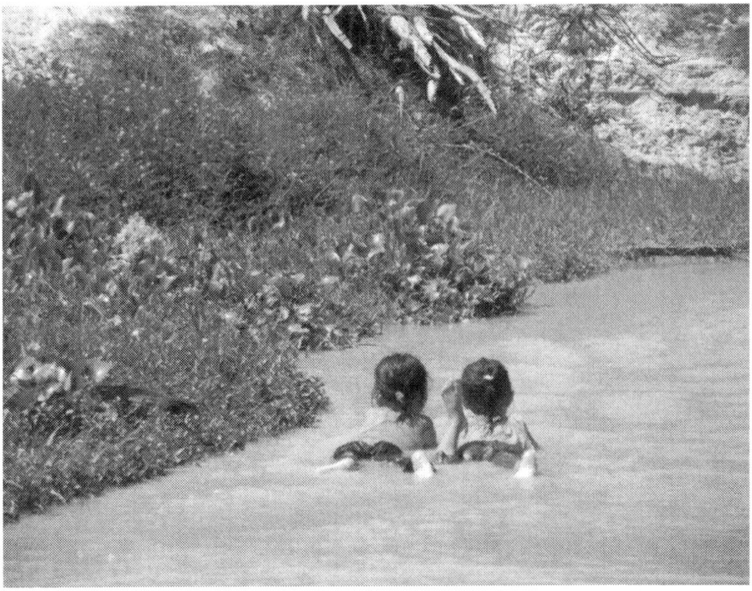

5.- Hoi An

Hoi An is just over an hour by plane from HCMC and it is an amazing place.

Just 20 minutes away from Danang by car, you will reach this beautiful fishing village that once used to be famous for its silk manufacturing.

With a huge influence of colonial France, the houses are absolutely beautiful, with many pedestrian roads.

Tranquillity, peace and something nice and different is waiting for you in Hoi An.

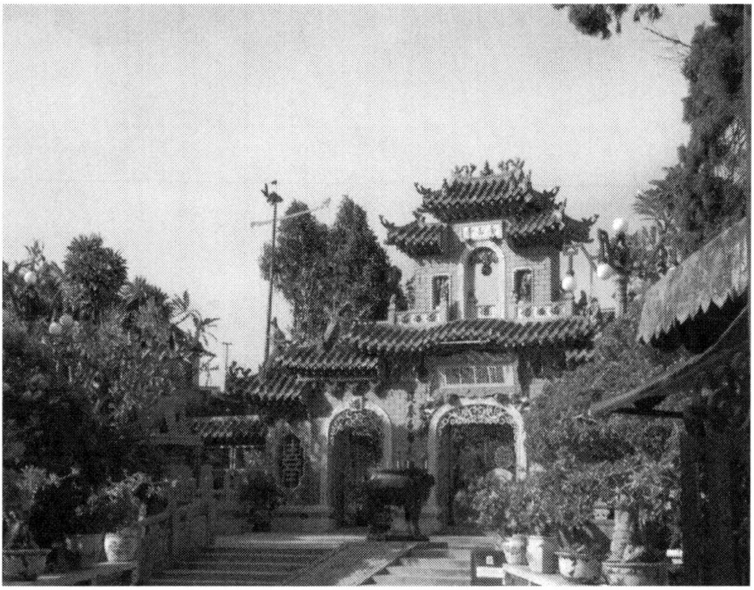

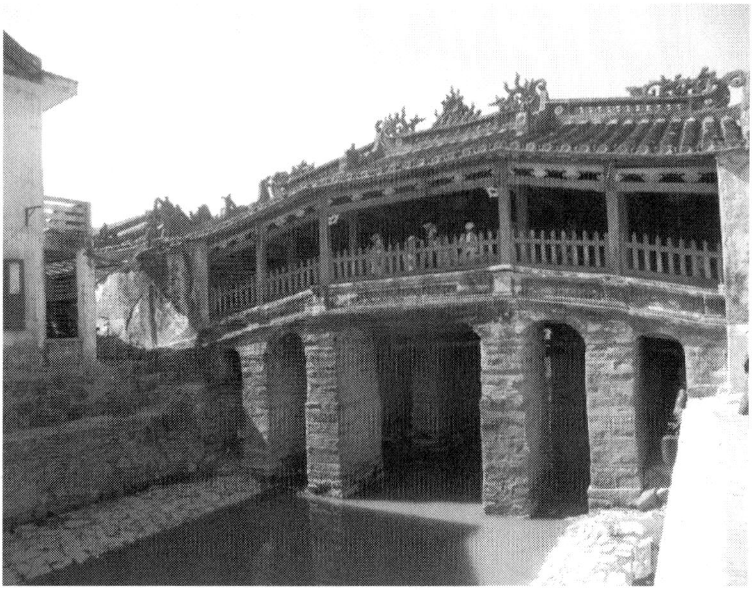

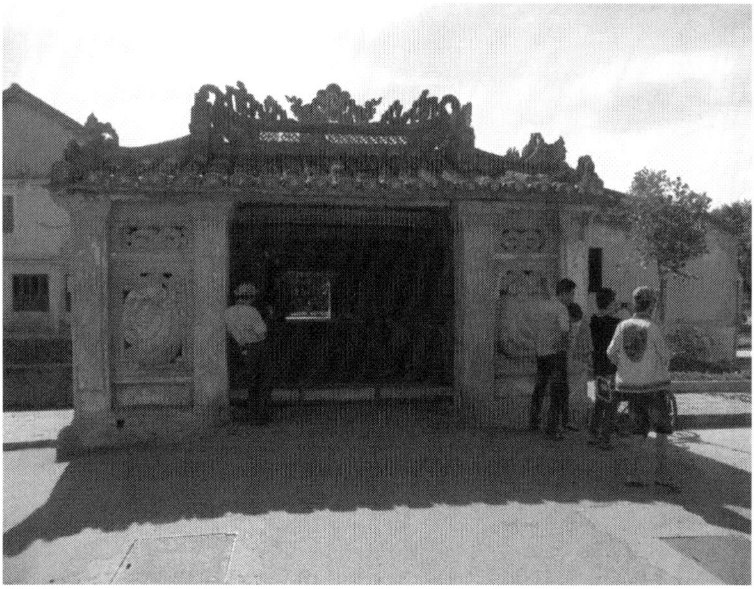

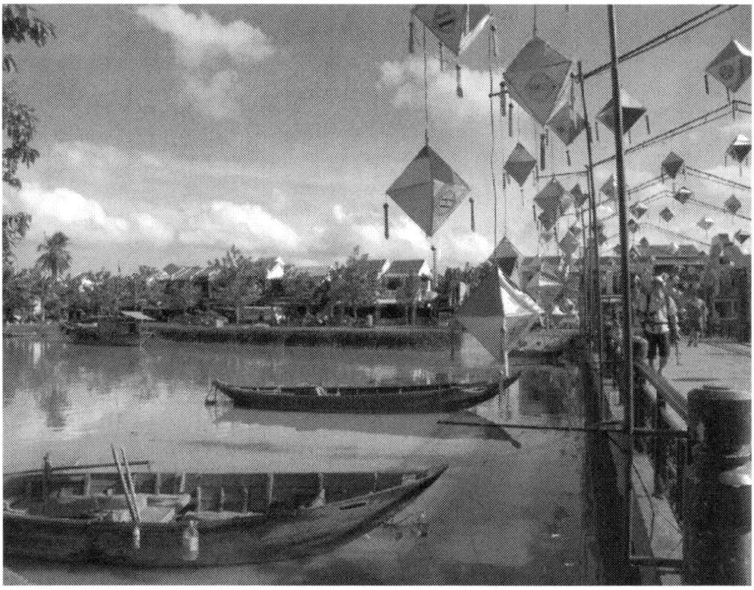

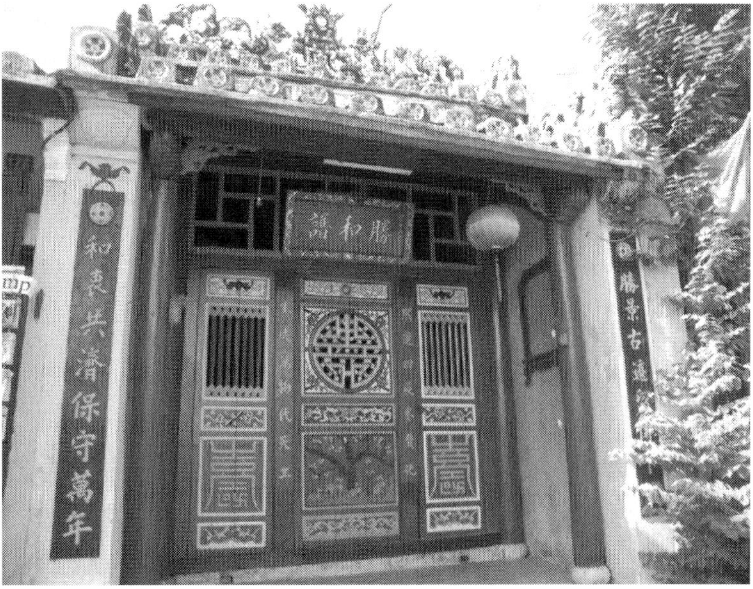
勝和舘
和東共濟保守萬年
勝景古

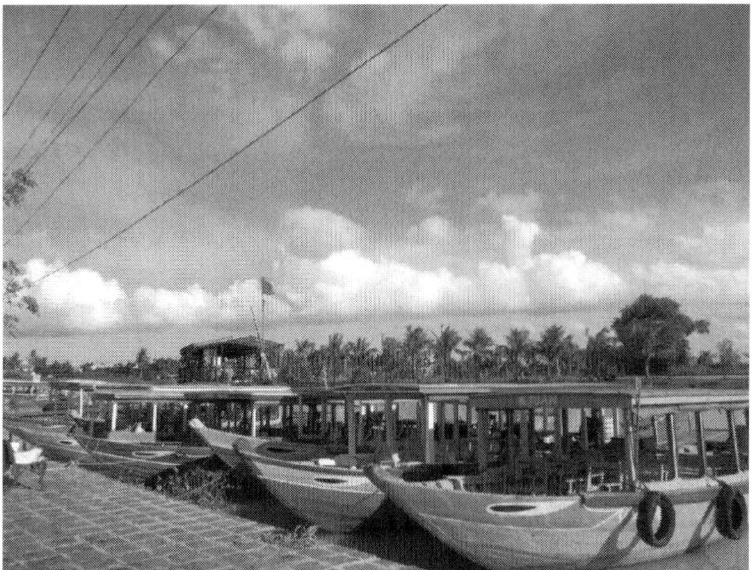

6.- Da Nang

Yet another place one hour away by plane from HCMC, Da Nang is busting with activity.

With more and more new bars and restaurants opening, is one of the more fasting developing cities.

Although it has its own beach, my best advice is that you book a resort in the beaches between Da Nang and Hoi An: you will benefit from better value for money, nicer beaches and better quality accommodation.

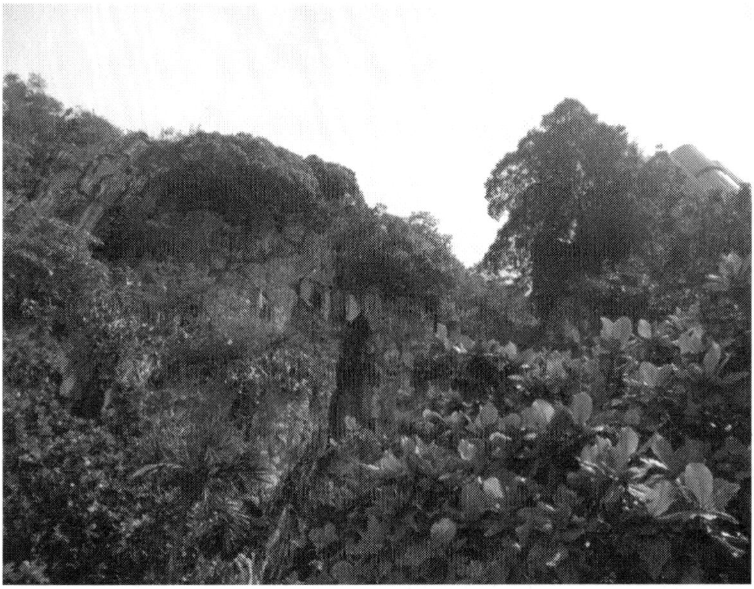

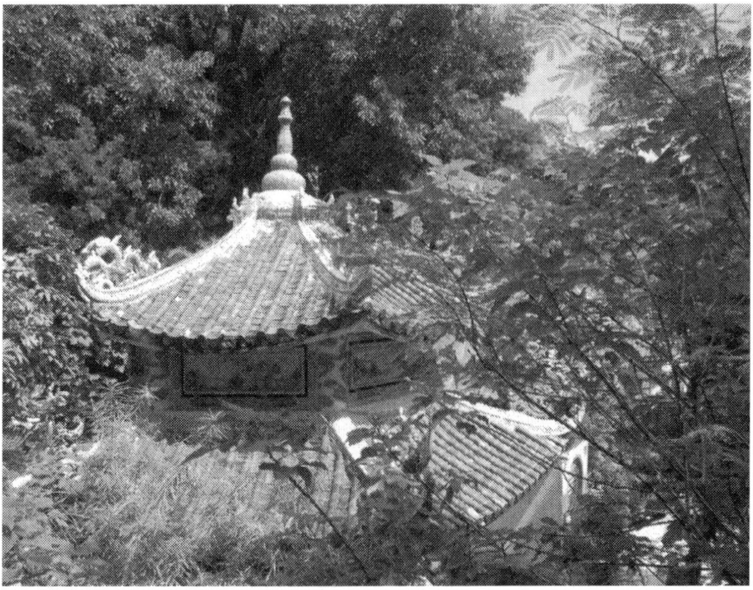

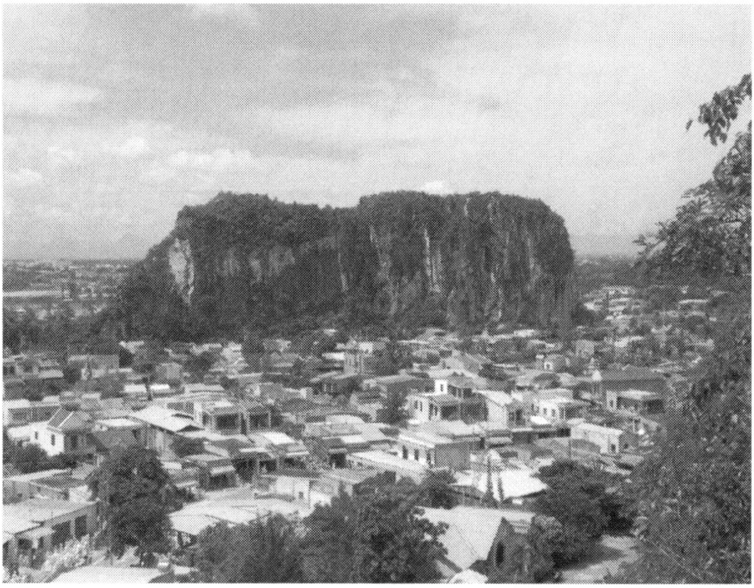

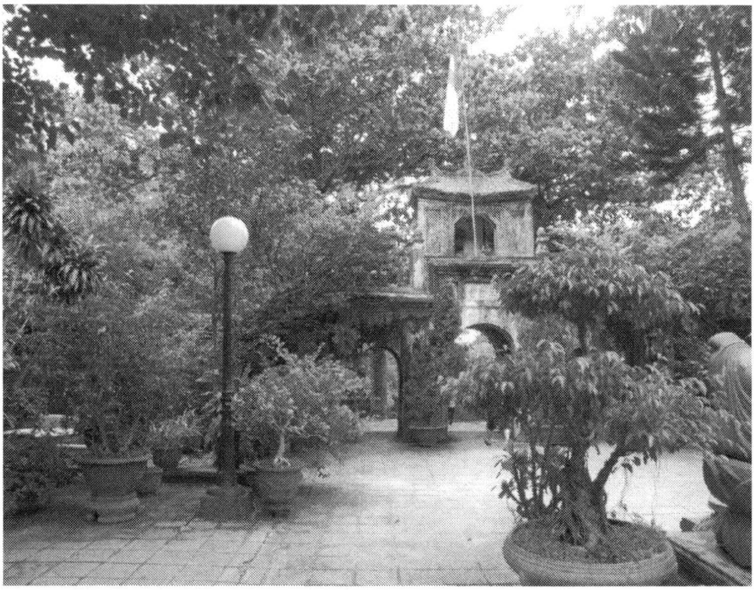

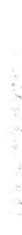

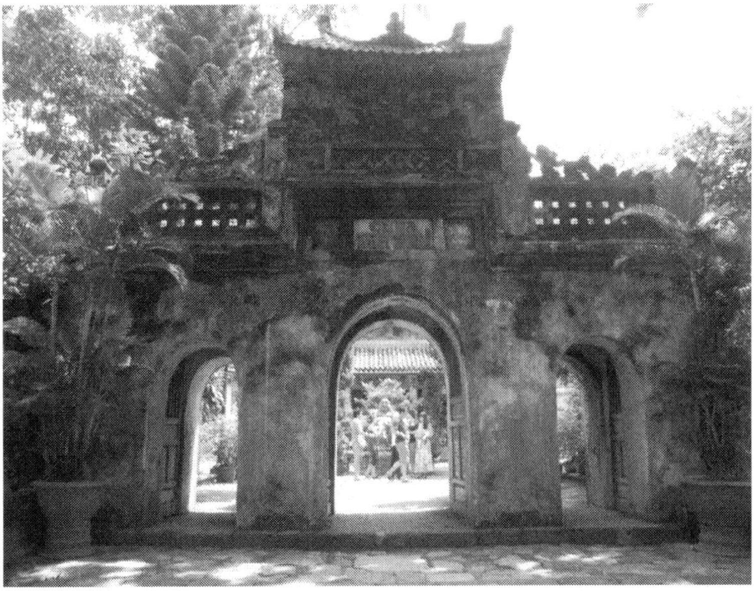

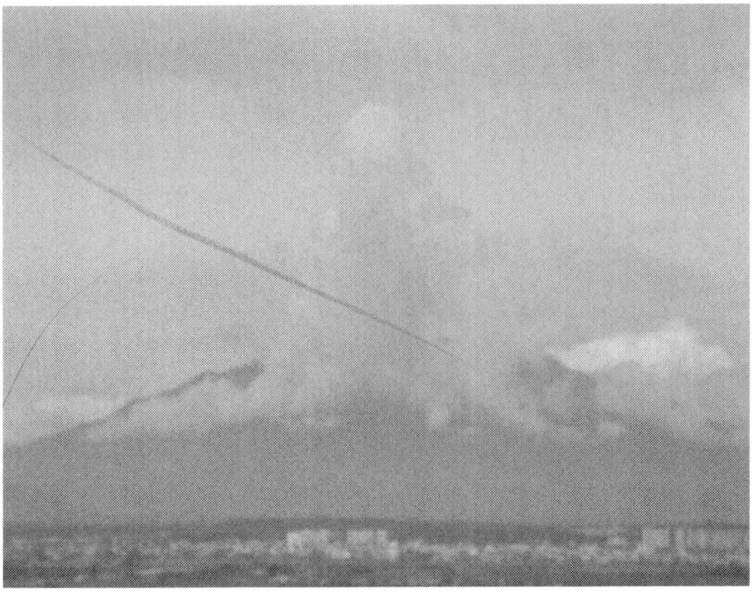

7.- Cu Chi

Cuchi is famous for the tunnels excavated there, which were used by the Vietcong during the war.

One of the most popular tourist attractions to those visiting HCMC, it is easy to be reached by different transport means, as it is just in the outskirts of HCMC.

Tip: try the river cruise taking you to Cuchi, very nice!

8.- Hue

Hue is spot on the middle of Vietnam. Just over one hour flight from HCMC, visit Hue if you are looking for a city full of history.

Hue is probably one of the most traditional towns in Viet Nam. Whatever you do, you must dedicate half day to visit the old citadel and royal palace, which are just amazing.

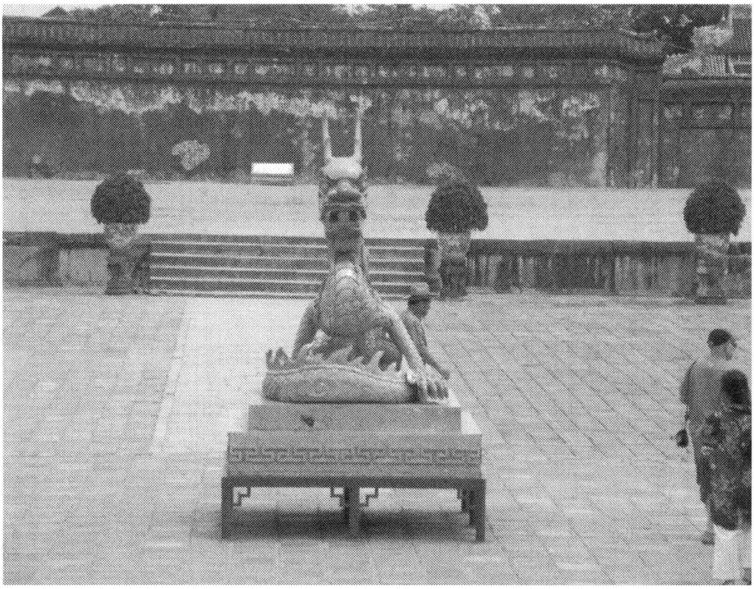

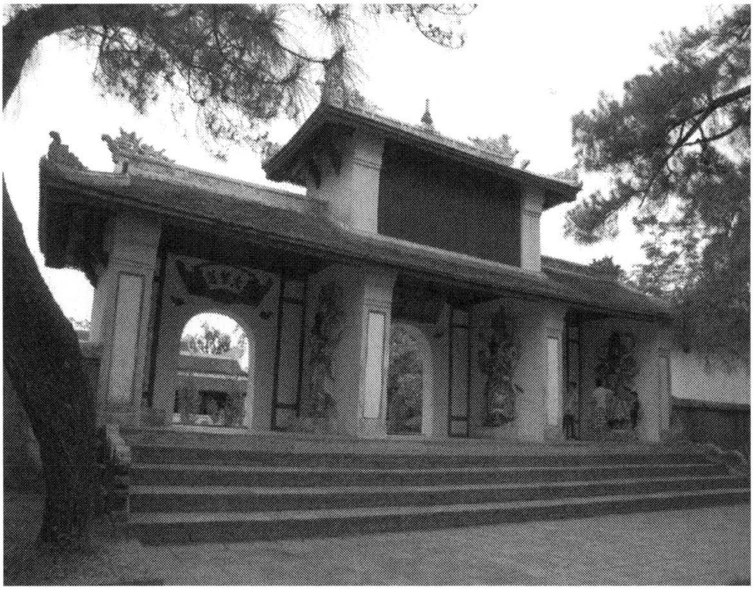

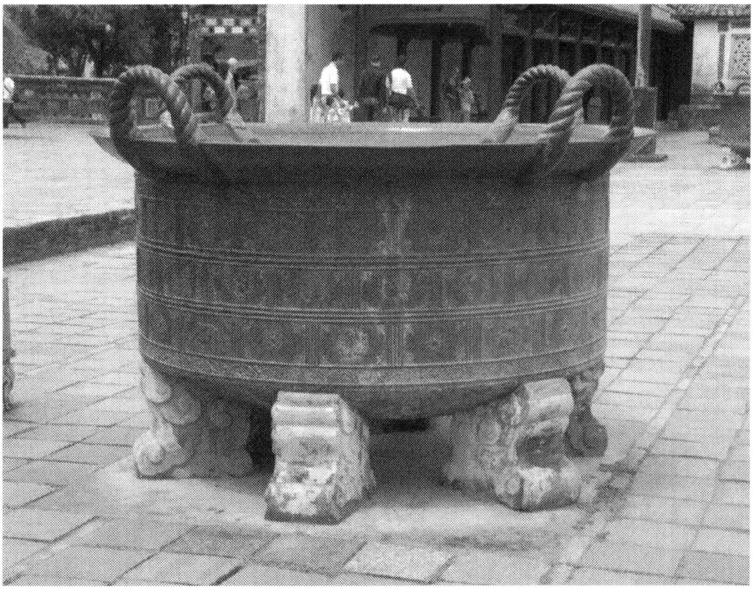

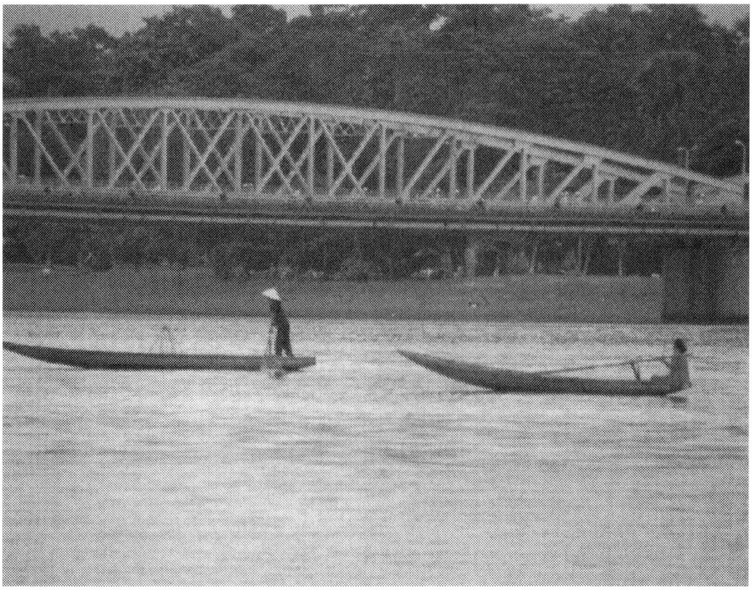

9.- Lagi

Lagi is somehow in between Mui Ne and HCMC, around 3-4 hours by coach will take you there, with many daily coaches available from HCMC.

A hidden jewel, still to be developed with very little tourism bringing both pros and cons: you can easily find virgin beaches where apart from vegetation and a couple of fishermen you will find no one, however very limited night life and resorts.

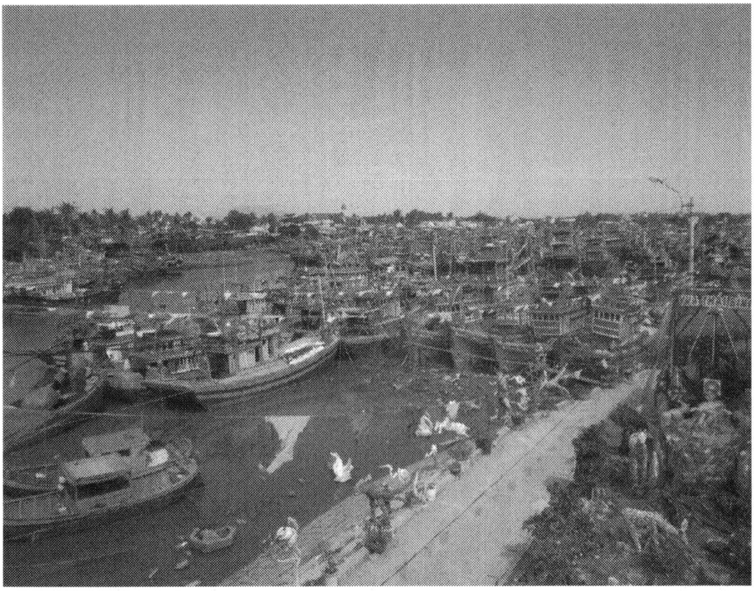

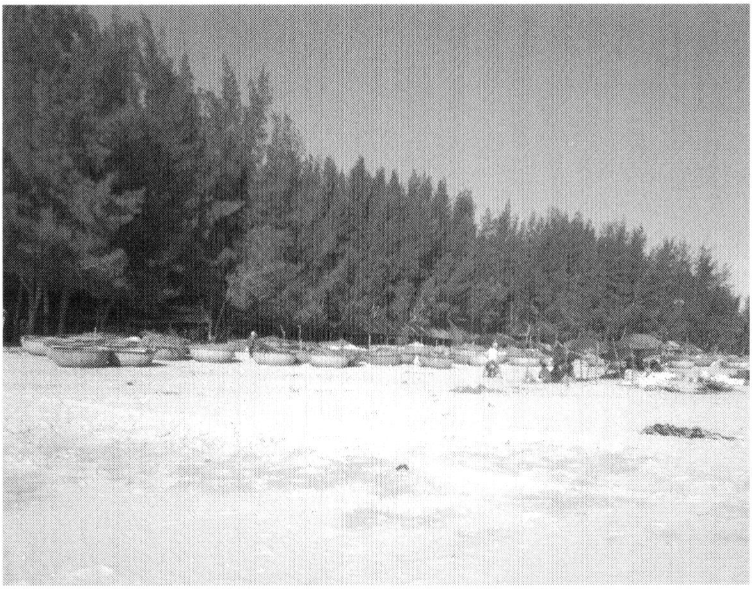

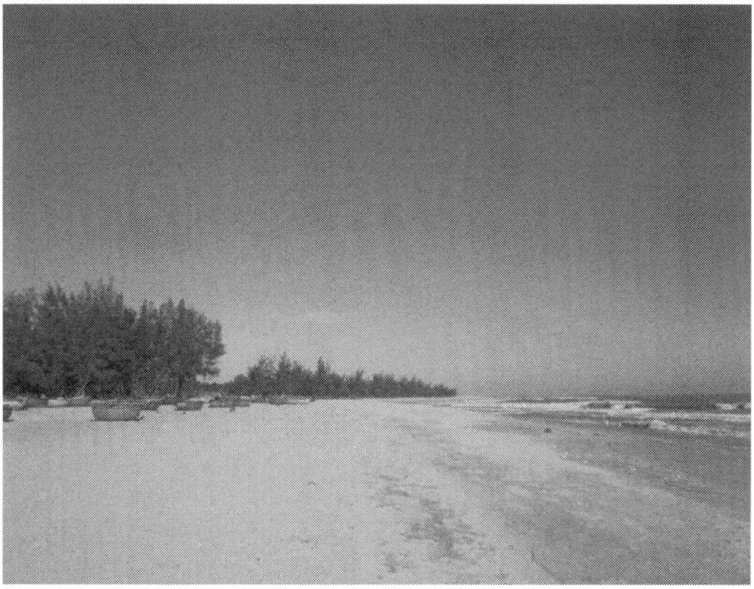

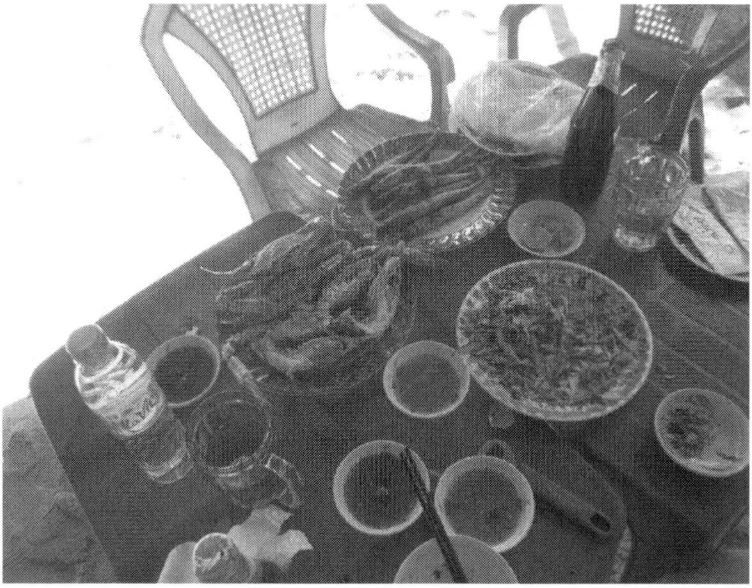

10.-Ha Noi

The capital is just under two hours by flight, with many daily flights from HCMC from different airlines.

Although more beautiful than HCMC due to the wider roads, avenues, parks and many trees, your experience will surely be negative affected by the terrible behaviour of many of the Northerners.

You just need a couple of days to visit Ha Noi, but you can have an extended break and visit typical places like Sapa, Halong Bay or Dinh Binh.

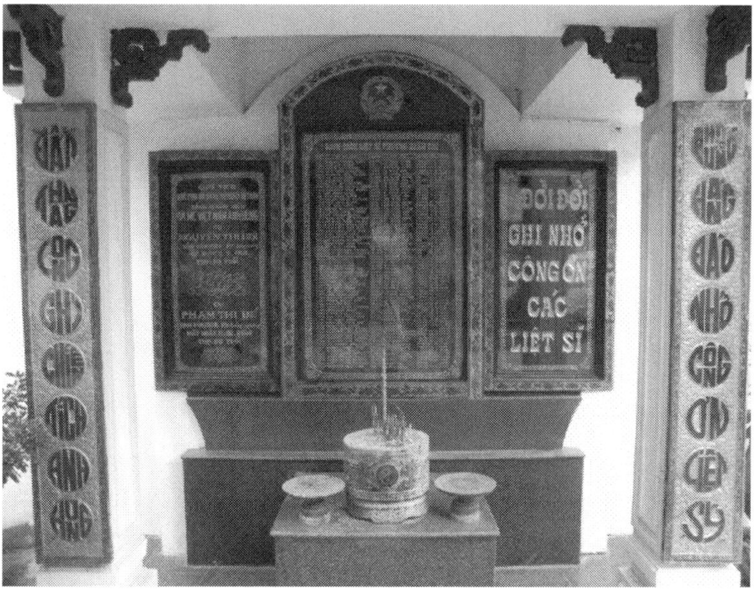
ĐỜI ĐỜI
GHI NHỚ
CÔNG ƠN
CÁC
LIỆT SĨ

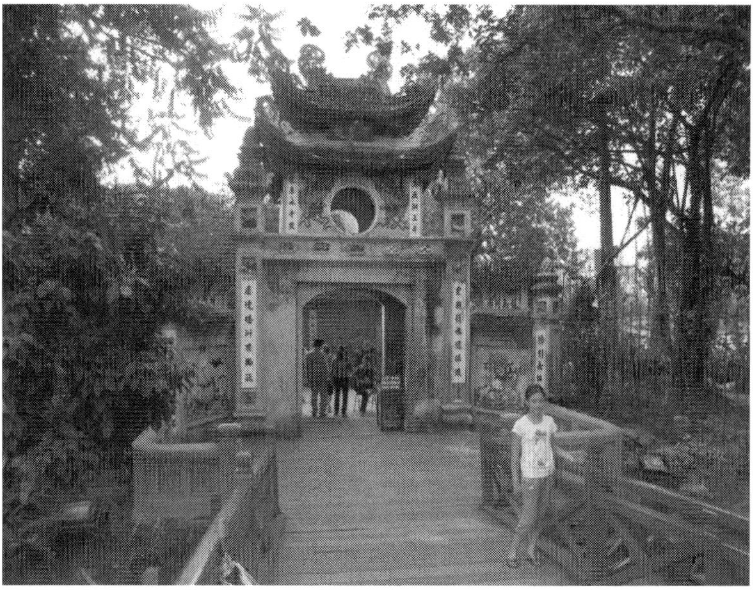

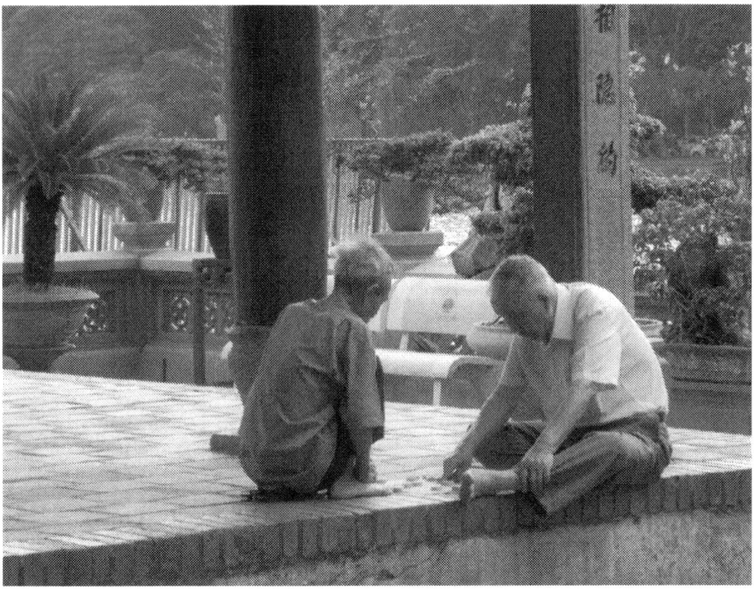

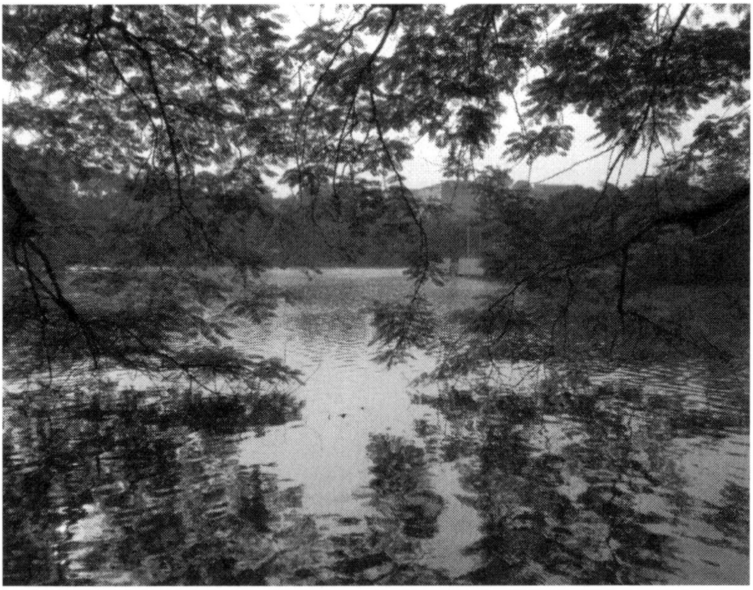

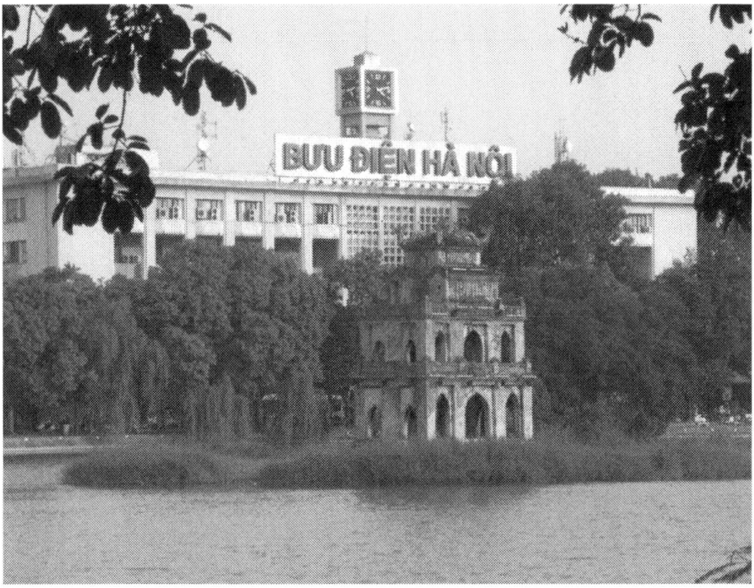
BƯU ĐIỆN HÀ NỘI

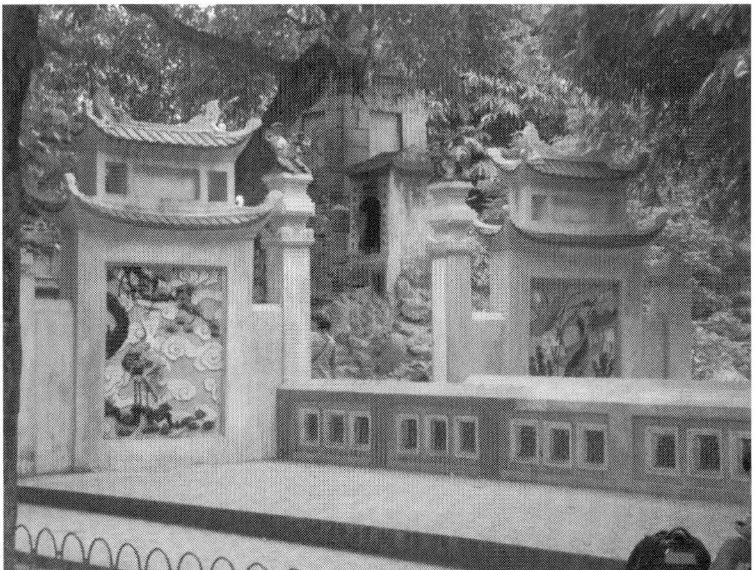

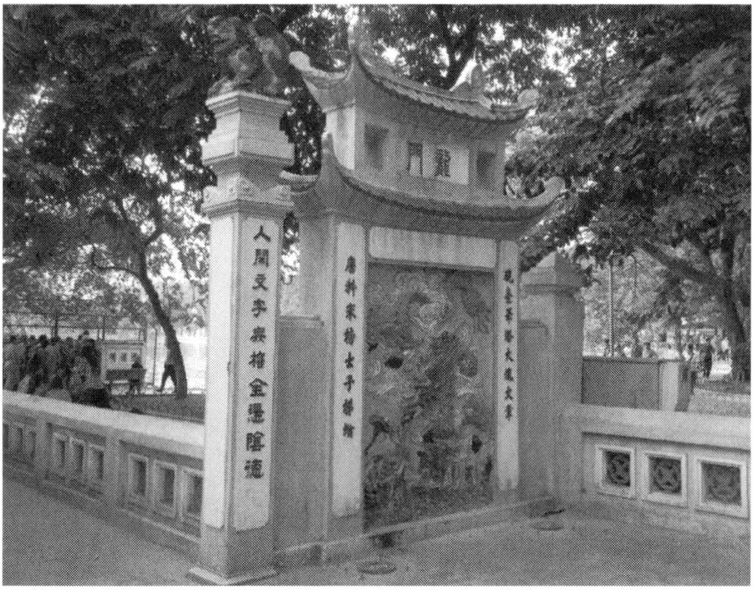

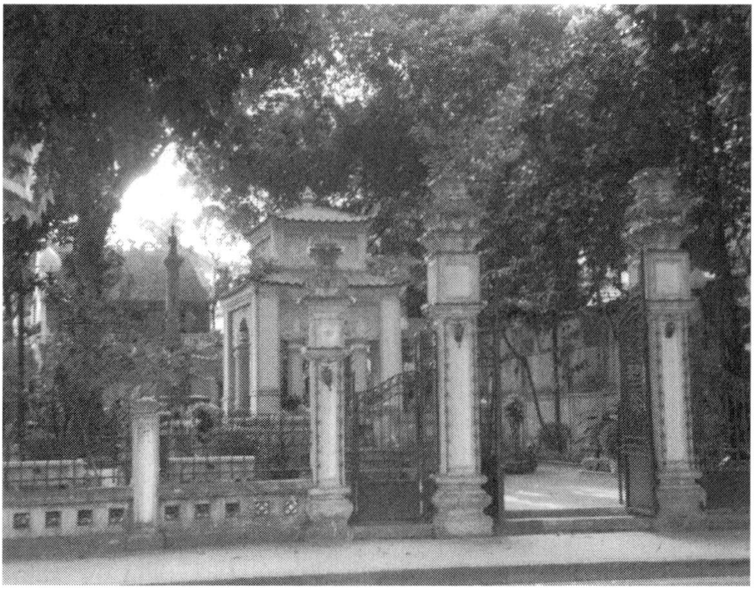

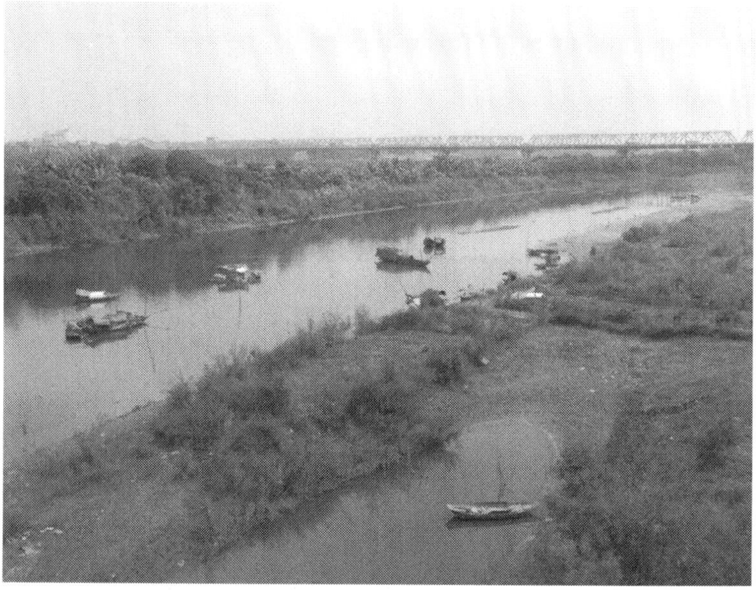

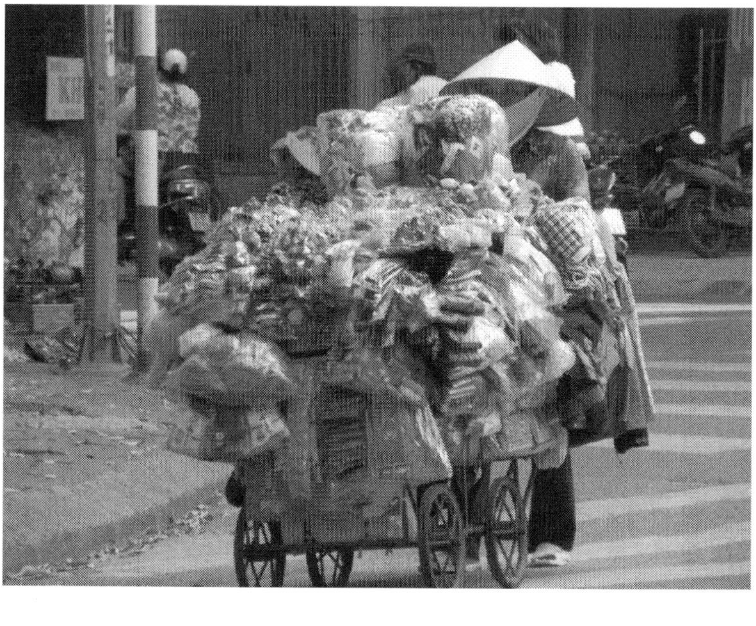

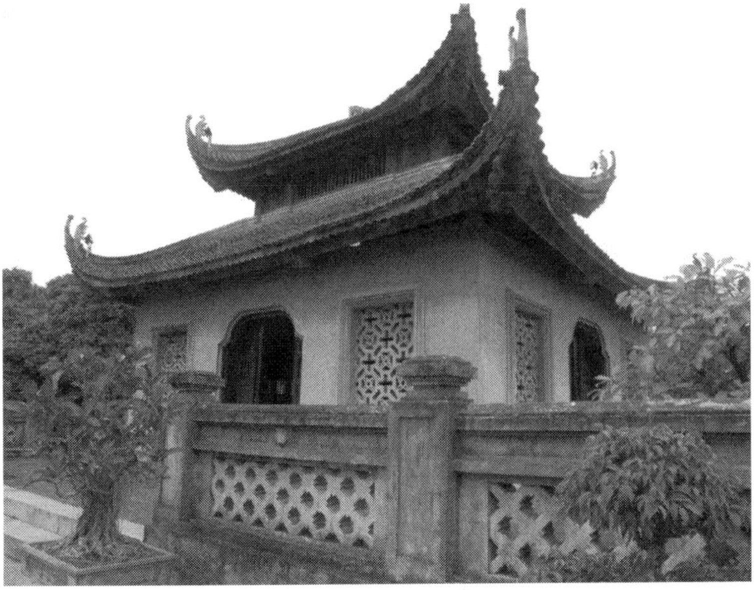

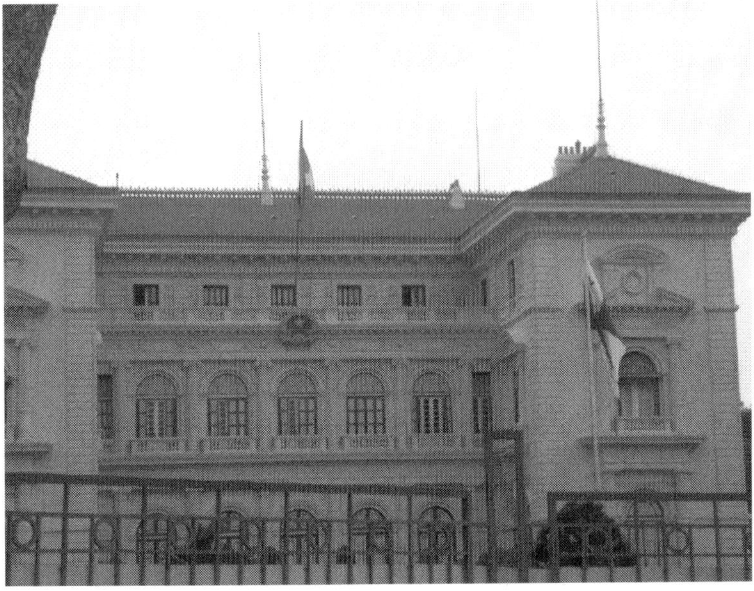

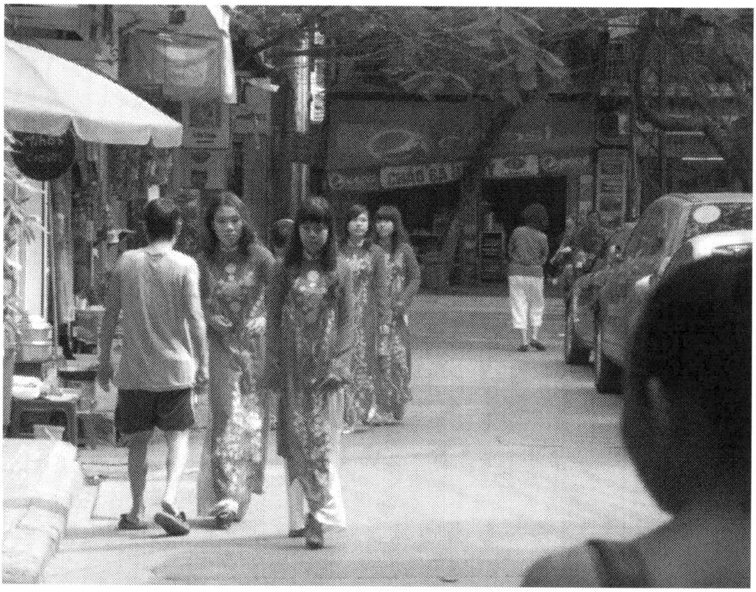

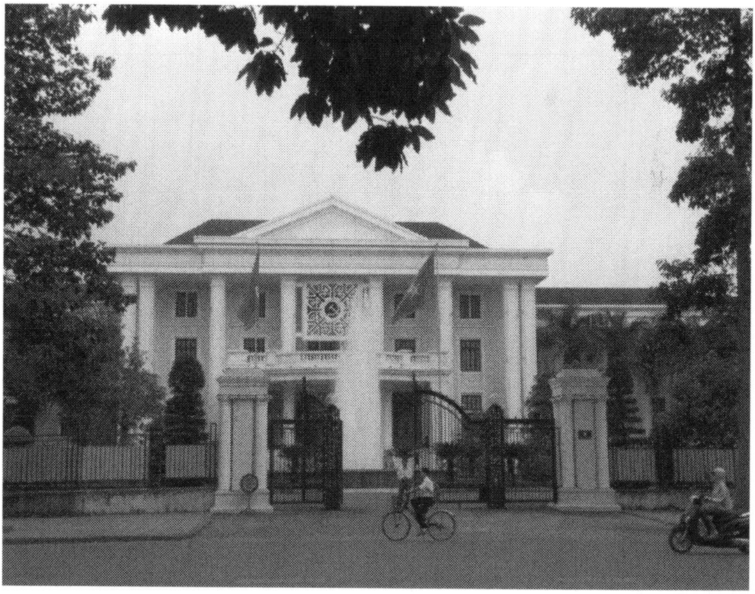

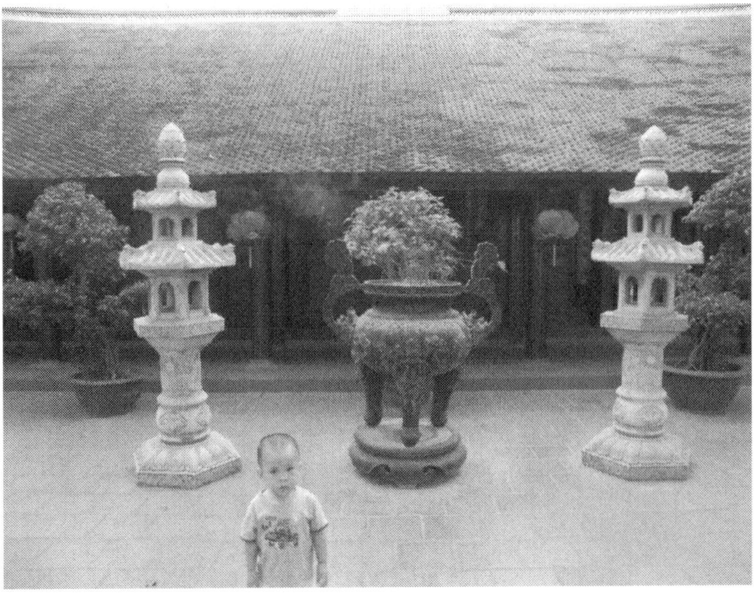

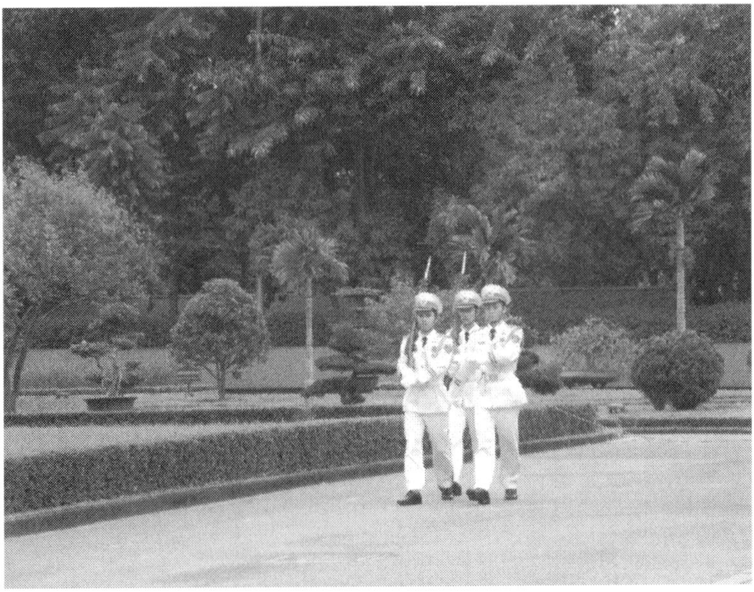

Top 10 What to buy

1.- Coffee

Vietnam is currently the largest coffee producer (robusta bean) in the world.

If you are a coffee lover, you will find lots of varieties here. However you must watch out and ensure that what you are buying is actually coffee.

After a few decades of hard times, where Vietnamese had to do anything to make ends meet, including mixing corn and green beans with coffee to increase the yield, several companies has developed the "skills" to produce coffee out of no coffee beans by using several chemical processes.

If you want to be safe buy coffee from Highlands coffee cafes or at Anam Gourmet market.

2.- Pepper

Vietnam produces some of the best pepper in the world.

Although most of the top quality production is currently being sported, it is not difficult to find, decent quality at rather low prices in the local markets and supermarkets.

3.- Ao dai

The Ao dai is the traditional Vietnamese dress for women, very beautiful and light, making women look even more sexy and radiant.

There are lots of shops selling aodais and if you have the time, you can just buy the material and get a local tailor to make one for you in around one week.

4.- Cashew nuts

Another of Vietnam's biggest exports are cashew nuts, producing some of the finest in the world.

Like with pepper the best quality is usually exported as it gets producers higher prices, however it is very easy to find good value for money cashews in any market or supermarket

5.- High cocoa content chocolate

Although not for very long, Vietnam is now producing good quality chocolate.

If you want dark pure, or high cocoa content chocolate, shop around for local varieties of chocolate and be amazed with the flavours.

6.- Exotic fruit

Even though I have travelled all over the world, it has been Vietnam where I have discovered and enjoyed lots and lots of new exotic fruits: yellow water melon, green oranges, sanpochea, …

Go to one of the local markets and enjoy the local fruits which are usually very cheap and delicious.

7.- Fish sauce

I personally hate it, actually I hate it very much but if you like or use fish sauce, you are in the right country as Vietnam is the largest producer, and probably largest user of fish sauce.

Go to any supermarket and choose from over 30 or 40 different varieties.

8. – Paintings

There are many local galleries and shops offering the works of local artists as well as reproductions for famous painters at reasonable prices.

If you like art, you cannot leave HCMC without visiting Liqhouse in District one. The gallery in the first floor offers amazing works of art, and in the ground floor you have a huge selection of international spirits and wines to choose from.

9.- Crocodile goods

Vietnam has many crocodile farms, and several companies offer great quality crocodile skin products: from shoes to wallets, but also handbags and belts, which you can find a rather reasonable prices.

10.- Fake goods

Ok, not that I suggest you buy them, but Vietnam is paradise for buying fake t-shirts, bags, clothing, shoes,... virtually everything.

Remember you are buying the brands much much cheaper, but you are not actually buying the same product, so don't be surprised if your new North Face bag falls into pieces after the first week!

"Top 10 places to drink"

1.- Caravelle Hotel

19-23 Lam Son Square, D1

This is probably the best hotel in HCMC. If you like independently run hotels, offering amazing customer services and all the facilities you need, Caravelle Hotel is for you.

Situated in the heart of Saigon, it is walking distance from the Opera House, the Post Office, the Town Hall and many other of the top attractions.

With several bars and restaurants, the roof top bar offers the joy of latin music from a Cuban band. Two more reasons not to miss the roof top bar are the incredibly well prepared cocktails and the city views.

2.- Sheraton Hotel

Dong Khoi, D1

Sheraton hotel is located in the centre of Saigon, not far from the many tourist attractions like Notre Dame Cathedral, the Post Office and the Opera House.

Set in a side road to one of the most famous shopping streets in Saigon, it offers the usual high quality standards typical of the Sheraton Hotel chain.

The rooftop bar offers live music, incredible city views and a good selection of cocktails and other beverages.

3.- Vino

Vino is just off Hai Ba Trung, and although the main business is selling wine, they offer a nice terrace where you can eat some delicious tapas.

There are several wines offered by the glass, however the highlight is, that you can choose any bottle from the shop, and with a rather small corkage charge, enjoy any of the many wines available.

4.- Pacharan

95 Hai Ba Trung, D1

Located in the heart of district 1, walking distance from the Opera house and other amenities, Pacharan is the top Spanish restaurant in Saigon.

Whether you want to go for some tapas or a la carte menu, you will not be disappointed. Nor will you with the amazing Spanish wine list, cocktails and offering one of the best served beers on tap in Saigon.

Wednesdays, Fridays and Saturdays are even more interesting due to live music on the first floor, offering an incredible environment, great music and drinks.

6.- Zan Z Bar

41 Dong Du, D1

Zanzibar is a modern mix of restaurant, wine bar and club.

Usually frequented by expats and Vietnamese alike, Zanzbar offers a vast wine and drinks list at up market prices.

7.- Blanchy's Tash

95 Hai Ba Trung, D1

Blanchy's Tash opened not long ago, and seems to be a real success with foreigners and locals alike.

Split over three floors, it mixes a lounge with a restaurant and different international DJs playing hip music.

Also known as the Ibiza of Saigon, if you are after something new, this is the place to be.

8.- Hoa Vien Brauhaus

28 D Mac Dinh Chi, D3

This restaurant and beer garden is in fact a microbrewery.

People come here to drink and eat, offering Czech and Bavarian style food as well as several types of Czech beer, be assured to have a great time, as well as great rich food and even better beer.

9.- Gammer

107 Pasteur, D1

This is another microbrewery in Saigon offering not only great pilsner beer but also a large selection of local and international food.

The place is huge, with tables over several floors as well as outside seating, nevertheless it tends to get rather fool.

Service is hot and miss though from ok to terrible, especially as what food is concerned, so be patient and don't complain and expect confrontational staff.

10.- Phan Xich Long

Phan Xich Long, Phu Nhuan

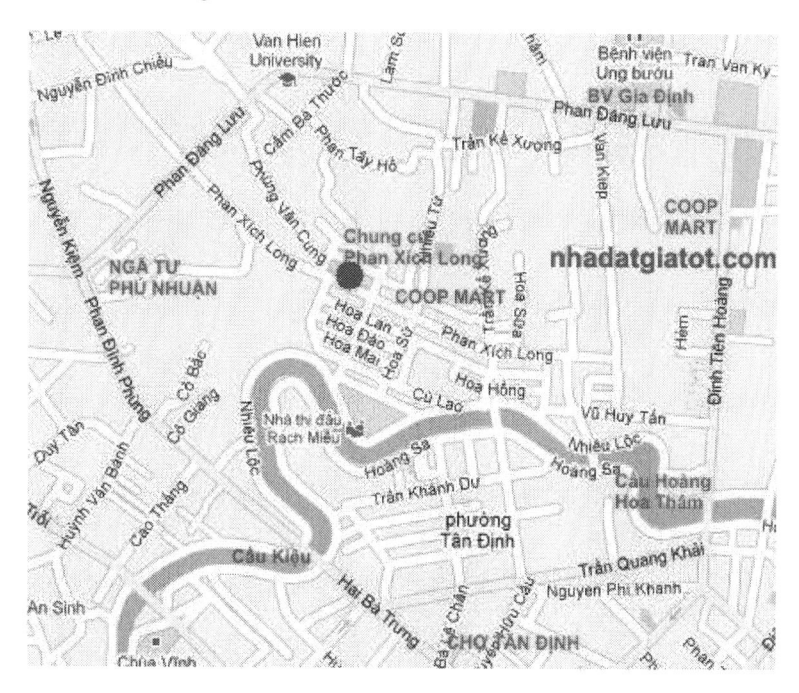

This is an area not far from District 1.

Once there walk around the small streets by the river and enjoy not only delicious food but also many places offering local beers for around $0.50 a bottle, expect to be seated in a plastic chair and get the curious looks of locals, as this is not a touristic place at all, but great food, cheap beer and overlooking the river.

Top 10 what to bring

1.- Antiseptic cream

Be aware that if you need it, and you are likely to do so, antiseptic cream is not available in Vietnam, as most locals will leave any minor injuries untreated.

2.- Mosquito repellent

If you expect to spend all or most of your holiday in HCMC, you should not fear the mosquitoes apart from annoying you a bit.

However if you visit the Mekong and/or rural areas, I strongly recommend that you bring a strong mosquito repellent and use it especially dusk and dawn. Although malaria is rare, dengue happens relatively often.

3.- Crucial medicines you need to take

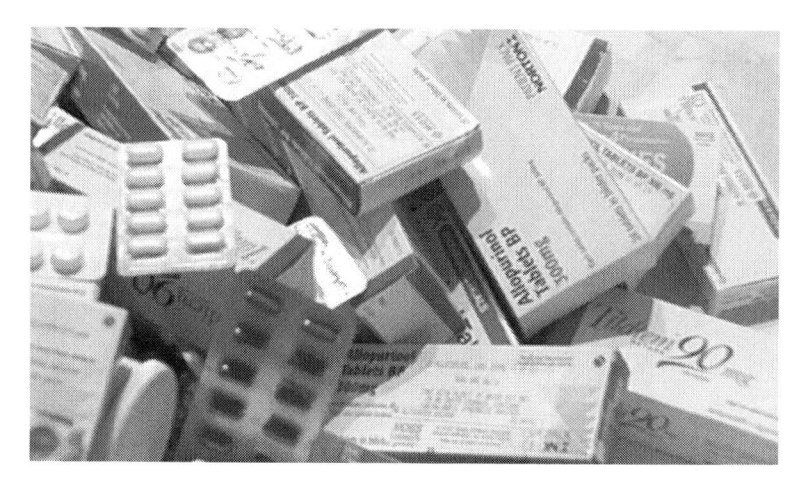

Although this is obvious for any country you visit, in Vietnam is particular important as many medicines which for us westerners are basic, are difficult to find or you may end up with fake Bangladeshi ones.

On the other hand, here you can find virtually everything, from antibiotics to codeine, without prescription.

4.- Shaving foam

Vietnamese men have very little facial hair, and therefore next to no need to shave on a regular basis. As a result shaving foam or gels are difficult to find, apart from some few big supermarkets. The same applies to aftershave creams.

On the other hand, razors are widely available.

Tip: if you forget and you are in an emergency go to one of the top shopping centres for top brands.

5.- Sun protection cream

Vietnamese don't like sun and like even less having dark skin, however rather than using sun block, they just cover themselves with as many clothes as possible, regardless of the very hot weather.

If you are desperate for sun protection cream, visit one of the big supermarkets, and you will be able to access a very limited and expensive range.

6.- Electricity plug converter

Vietnamese use both American (two plate pins) and European two round pins (not UK) international plug systems.

In many hotels you will find plugs accepting both systems, however bring a plug converter just in case, or if you are traveling from the UK.

7.- Copies of passport and key documents

Hopefully nothing will happen to your original documents, but if it does, you will save a lot of time and frustration if you have copies to present to your embassy or consulate to get new ones.

8.-Big size underwear

If like me you use XL or higher underwear, expect to find none here, as it is very difficult to find Vietnamese using such large size, so I recommend as many clothes as you need.

T-shirts can be found of any size.

9.-Condoms

If you are planning to use them, bring your own!

Condoms are widely available, however you are likely to face two problems: fake imports from China, and size, to cater for the local population.

10.- Rechargeable batteries

If you want to keep environment clean and/or save the environment, you may want to use rechargeable batteries for your camera, etc.

Although normal batteries are easy to find in Vietnam, rechargeable ones are rather difficult and only in some touristic areas at inflated prices) and few big supermarkets.

Top 10 Language

1.- Yes: vang

2.- No: Khong

3.- Hello: Xin chao

4.- Thank you: Cam on

5.- Bye: Tam biet

6.- English: tieng anh

7.- Expensive: mac qua

8.- Water: nuoc

9.- Beer: bia

10.- Restaurant: nha hang

Practical Information Top 10

1.- Visas and Arrival

Visa requirements change continuously, therefore independently of what I write here, I strongly recommend that you check with the Vietnamese Embassy what are the current requirements for your nationality.

There are several types of Visa, and depending the reason why you are coming to Viet Nam, can be simplified into two types: work and tourism.

Work Visas are complicated and tedious, very complicated. Most importantly, you can not have a work Visa if you do not have a job offer, followed by a work permit and for you to have a work permit, it has to be arranged by your employer... yes kind of catch 22, but everything is possible in Viet Nam...

So you are looking at coming to Viet Nam without a working visa or a work permit, my best advice is that you get a three month tourist visa, and once in the country, your employer should arrange for the work permit and then the residence permit (so that you do not need a visa any more).

There are two ways to obtain your visa: the traditional way of going to your local Vietnamese consulate, which takes time, or arrange for a visa on arrival over the internet and then get the visa once you arrive to Viet Nam, which is what I recommend.

Patience is a skill you should develop, and you will notice this as soon as you touch ground in the country. Even if you have your visa on arrival arranged, you will have to wait, at least 30 minutes, for getting the proper paper visa attached to your passport; then go through security control and then through customs control once you have collected your luggage.

Important! Keep your luggage tickets with you all the time until your leave the airport, as in most airports they will check that the luggage you are carrying corresponds with the number in your ticket, therefore no luggage ticket big problem!

2.- Buying and loading a local simcard

Have I ever mentioned that there are two ways of... doing things in Viet Nam? Of course, for virtually everything!

Well you can go to the branch of one of the shops of the major Vietnamese mobile operators and buy it there for which you will have to provide your passport/ residence card, fill some forms and after 30 to 60 minutes get your sim card ready to operate.

Option two is to go to one of the many shops and buy a sim card and start using it, which is what I would recommend. Another good thing about doing this is that the seller is likely to inform you about the different offers and help you choose the company that best suit you.

3.- Shopping for food and basic goods

Supermarkets, especially big ones like Coop Mart and Big C, have only recently appeared in the Vietnamese scene with most shopping traditionally done in markets and local shops.

Each city and town, depending on size, will have one or several local markets which are usually open from the very early morning until 5-6 in the afternoon. In these there is an array of different food but also other things like clothing, kitchenware. The important thing is, regardless of what you are buying, with very few exceptions, expect to bargain a lot or pay an overprice.

The same applies to most local shops, where by the simple fact of you being a foreigner, or even locals with accents from other regions, will automatically turn into a price increase which in some cases will multiply tenfold.

In Viet Nam virtually every home will be turned into a shop or restaurant in their basement, especially if they are located in a main road. Vietnamese have an astonishing gift for entrepreneurship as it can be reflected in the thousands of businesses open everywhere.

The new supermarkets, like everywhere else in the world, are proving a real success. They carry a large selection of goods, prices may be slightly more expensive than in markets and shops, but not always, but food quality tends to be much better. Fresh product may not be so tasty as in markets, but there definitely much more safer.

Some supermarkets like Big C accept payment by credit card, but most don't, although this is changing fast.

4.-Safety

Viet Nam is usually a safe place even big cities, there is no major crime. However there is an increasing tendency to be robbed while driving your motorbike, especially if you are a woman or a foreigner.

You are more likely to become a victim of a crime if you are riding late at night, and/or carrying a handbag or backpack (they will assume you carry an expensive laptop), and or if you are in some rough districts in HCMC.

Just a few weeks ago one of my colleagues was attacked while driving a motorbike and they stole her bag containing her passport, credit cards, hard drive and a few more things. But she was driving late at night, not in a very good area, with a backpack and she is a foreigner female.

Overall as I mentioned before, crime is low, but watch out.

5.- Food

Vietnamese food is very varied, tasty and the secret is that is usually cooked using fresh ingredients only.

There are lots of regional variations and local dishes, however overall most dishes are either rice or rice noodle based, so if you are not familiar with using chopsticks, it is time to learn.

Many of the Vietnamese dishes are based on a noodle soup to which meat and/or fish are added. Some typical ones are Bum Bo Hue or Pho.

If you don't like bones or skin, make sure you specify that, as Vietnamese love the meat on bone, and even with the skin.

Grilled fish is absolutely delicious, widely available, cheap and fresh.

Seafood is amazing, especially if you are close to the see or in HCMC, and if you like snails, this is paradise.

Vietnamese eat virtually everything, and they love pork, so if you are Muslim or have any issues with pork, insist in no pork, as they like to put it with everything, including salads, spring rolls, vegetarian dishes.

There are some restaurants specializing in Vietnamese gourmet food, which are rather expensive, but feel free to try. Their specialties usually include grilled bugs, snake, roasted rice rat,...yummy!

Food sharing is very important in Viet Nam, and is a great part of socializing, so expect to see big groups in restaurants.

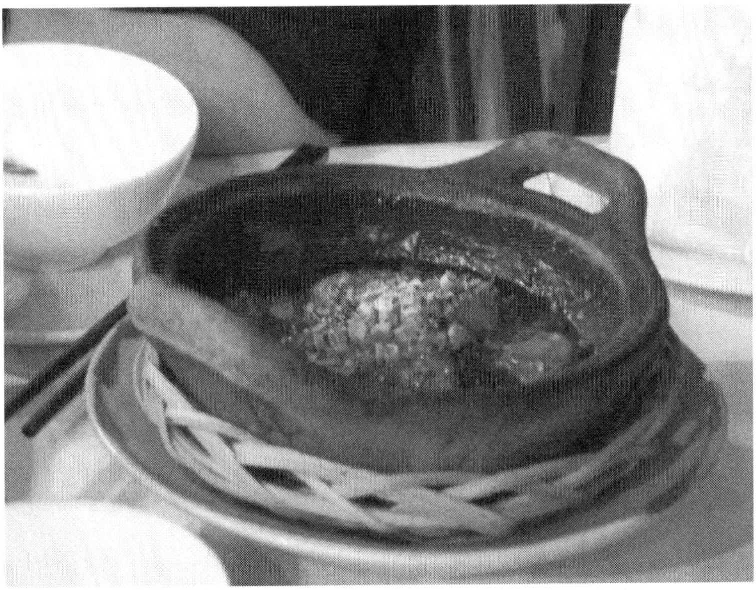

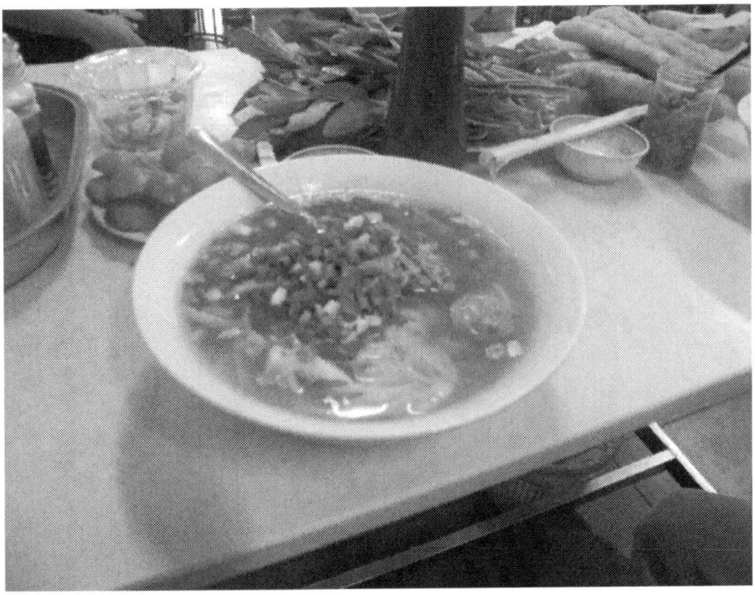

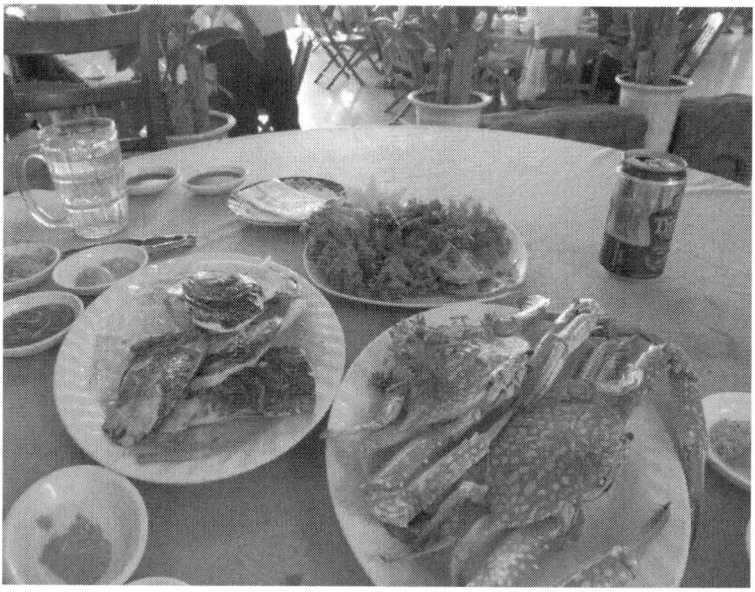

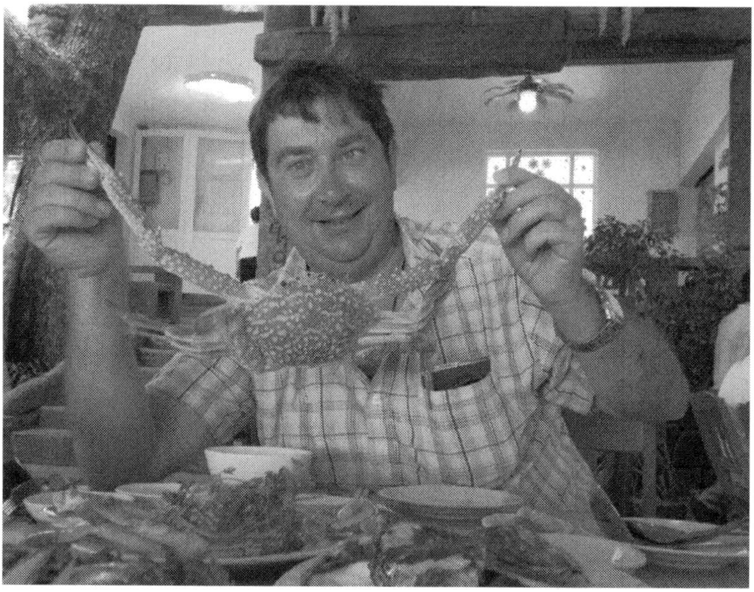

6.- Smoking

Although in general Vietnamese do not smoke a lot, smoking is allowed everywhere and is very common, so even if top restaurants, expect your table neighbors to be smoking…and there is not much you can do.

Usually the worst offenders are foreigners, who first find tobacco here so cheap that they over indulge their lungs with tobacco to get closer and quicker to lung cancer death; secondly they take this as an opportunity to do what is forbidden in their own countries and smoke during a meal or while having drinks.

7.-Rain

As Forrest Gump used to say there are many types of rain in Viet Nam, and it is true and if they have something in common is that all of them will get you wet!

So today started with big rain, so what do you do? If you have to work, you need to find your way there, the good is that around half of the usual motorbikes are not there, the other half drive much more slowly, but there are three times more cars (whose drivers do not have a clue on how to drive in rain), roads are flooded (so it is more difficult to drive the motorbike and you can not see the many potholes), plus the idiots driving next to you will not realize that if they speed cross a pond they will virtually shower you with dirty water, nice!

So if you have the choice, don't leave your apartment. If you must leave well consider taking a taxi, which are not easy to find in rain, and which will take three times longer than usual to arrive.

If neither of the above options is an option, well, you better have a huge good rain coat, patience and be prepared to get wet…very wet…so I advise you wear slippers and you carry some dry clothes and a towel with you so you can change on arrival.

8.- Tips

Tipping is not common in Viet Nam, with very few exceptions, however the large affluence of American tourist have taught the Vietnamese of this horrible business of tipping, and in some places is now expected and you maybe even get an angry face if you don't.

I am against tipping, you pay for a product or a service and that's it, and nothing describes better my thoughts that the first few minutes of the film Reservoir dogs, if you like tipping, why you don't tip in McDonalds?

Anyway, here you will find that most people don't expect tips, and in many occasions when I have decided to leave a tip the waitress has run after me thinking I had forgotten my money!

There are a couple of exceptions though: massage, where girls have a low salary and make most of their money via tips; and hairdressers where they expect a small tip for the service.

9.- Hospitals, doctors and dentists

If you have not done yet, get health insurance quick! Even if your health is fine and you have no issues, it is a matter of time before you need to access healthcare, and it will be sooner than you think.

It is hardly any day I don't see a road/motorbike accident, is not so much how well you drive but the others...even if you are being driven or walking as a pedestrian (not long ago I saw a couple of westerners being driven over in a zebra crossing in the center of Saigon...), and here people don't have insurance, and are very likely to run away, so if the worst happens you really want to have health insurance.

The same applies to food. I am very careful, I have travelled all over the world, I have a very strong stomach...but you just need a clam or a shrimp to be bad to start your misery. My first food poisoning lasted a week, the side effects a month...

So, if you need to go to hospital or see a doctor, you have three options:

Vietnamese state hospitals. You don't want to go there, believe me, they are full crowded, outdated, noisy and most important, it is unlikely that anyone will understand you unless you are fluent in Vietnamese, so not the best situation when you have a health issue.

Vietnamese private hospitals. These are usually modern, clean and all staff can speak English, well more or less, so you need to be careful: when I got food poisoned I went to my local private hospital that has a great reputation and is brand new. I explained my problem to the receptionist, I paid the consultant fee (yes you pay in advance), I was taken to the waiting room and I saw the doctor to who I explained my condition…she then asked me why I went to see her as she was a bone and fracture specialist…out again, taken to a different room and wait until I saw the right doctor, which is the last thing you need when you are suffering.

The experience was better, but watch out for common mistakes: I was given two medicines one to take with a little water the other with a liter of water…the nurse, who is the one who types the prescription and prints it wrote for both to be taken with a little water…so listen all the time.

Foreign hospitals. Here you are likely to have many foreign consultants and some Vietnamese educated abroad. They are more expensive but if your health is important, these are the places to visit. I will never forget when I had to go to one of the best foreign hospital for my health check in order to get my work permit and it was great, people speak proper English (sometimes French and German), it was like being in Europe.

If you plan to live in Viet Nam for some time and you can afford it, get a proper health insurance, mostly just in case something major happens. Be aware that if you came here with travel insurance, it is likely not to cover you once you have been here for 30 days, please don't mistake travel insurance with health insurance…they are very different!

Basic health is very cheap here even if you go to a private hospital; however if you need serious surgery or treatment, cost will escalate easily.

However if you are rarely ill, the best option is to go to one of the international hospitals, you pay more but you pay for what you get!

10.- Pharmacies

There are lots and lots of pharmacies in Viet Nam. You will see them, small in size, in virtually every street.

Some things you need to be aware when visiting a pharmacy are:

- English is not spoken in most of them.
- They have very limited supplies
- Most products are generic
- The qualified pharmacist is hardly ever there, and the people serving you may have zero medical qualifications, in some cases they just "buy" the pharmacy franchise from a qualified pharmacist.
- When you come with a prescription or ask for medication for a symptom, the pharmacist will get a combo-mix of tablets for you that she will cut in individual tablets (so forget about trying to read what is in the back of the blister).
- Don't expect to be given the prospectus unless you buy the full box, and even in these cases it is likely to be in Vietnamese.
- Pharmacist tend to give you a mix of everything… just in case. Last time I had a cough and cold I went to the pharmacy and I was given 3 daily doses for three days each containing 8 tablets. I did a little bit of research/detective work and I was given from antibiotics (which have no effect on

virus and should be taken for a minimum of 7 days) to allergy tablets... I must say it cured me though (maybe I got too scared of the tablets!)
- If the pharmacist does not understand you properly, he will give you something to treat what he thinks he understood: last time I was taken to a pharmacy by a Vietnamese colleague who translated for me (I was desperate with a cough) and I was given something for a sore throat rather than for a cough... be aware!
- Finally, some drugs are fake!

Some recommendations if you need to visit a pharmacy/use their services:

- Go to a doctor who speak English and get a prescription.
- International hospitals have wonderful pharmacies, they speak English and you know the drugs are not fake.
- Make sure they write for you the dose and frequency, even if in Vietnamese, you can get it translated (is not the same 3 every 8 hours than 8 every 3 hours...for them is easy to mistake when speaking in English.. I have lived it!)
- Unless you are one step from dying, in which case you should go to a hospital, before taking any medication given by the pharmacist get yourself in front of a

computer with internet connection, and research the generic component to make sure you have an idea of what are you about to take!

Some basic medicines, like antiseptic cream, are unknown here, so if you see the future need for them, bring plenty when you come. You can legally import medicines.

Top 10 mixing with the locals

1.- Tet Holiday customs and tradition

Tet is the Vietnamese lunar year, and dates vary each year as it follows the lunar calendar. It is probably the most important and meaningful time of the year for Vietnamese.

During this period that can last from a few days to a month, most people go back to their home towns to spend time with family; this is especially noticeable in big cities like HCMC or Hanoi, which seem deserted during Tet period.

If you are spending this time alone or just with foreigners, make sure that you stock up on food and drinks because everything will close, and I mean everything… or virtually everything: all shops, big supermarkets, restaurants, coffee shops… you may find the odd big international restaurant open, but not easy.

If you are spending time with Vietnamese, you must know the local customs and try to follow them:

Lucky money, which is their way of wishing luck for the New Year, is put in special envelopes and given to friends and relatives on the New Year. If you are visiting a family, you will be expected to give lucky money, especially to children. The amount of money you put inside is really up to you, but as orientation, around a dollar for children should be ok, and a minimum of three dollars for adults.

When you give the lucky envelopes don't expect them to open in front of you, although this may happen. Being a foreigner it is automatically assumed that you have more money than them, so higher amounts are expected and probably they will not give you any lucky money.

Tet is time to spend and visit different family members and be visited by them, so if you are with Vietnamese expect to be visiting the houses of different family members, and also be visited by them and in each occasion drink and eat a lot: sometimes tea, but mostly beer while wishing each other the best for the new year. Food varies from full huge meals to snacks (very sweet ones).

It is a lovely time, but it can be repetitive if you are not close to them and/or cannot speak Vietnamese, but it is highly recommended as a great experience.

2.- Coffee, coffee shops and locals

In case you did not know, Viet Nam is one of the largest producers of coffee in the world, and Vietnamese love coffee, as you will realize seeing how many coffee shops are around.

There is a huge difference in coffee quality between big cities and the countryside, in the latter you will notice a funny taste as they mix coffee with corn to get a better yield, let's say that it just tastes different.

It is very typical to drink black coffee with ice, and if you order the milk version expect it to be served with condensed milk.

Vietnamese love going to cafes as is their excuse to socialize. They usually spend hours chatting in cafes and don't be surprised to see that each of them usually orders just one drink during the time they spend there, remember their main reason to go there is not drinking coffee but socializing… when I raise this with some of them they told me that because Vietnamese coffee is so strong they need to drink it slowly ☺

The way locals drink coffee is by placing it in an aluminum container that works as a filter, adding hot water to it, then placing on top of a glass and wait for the coffee to filter one drop at a time. Requires time and patience…which goes well with the culture.

You will find two extremes when choosing where to go for coffee: the local shops where you are likely to have a plastic seat and table on the street and pay 33 cents for a coffee, or the various luxury western style cafes where you are likely to pay anything from $1 to $5 for a coffee, and much more for average food.

By the way, it is normal among Vietnamese that whoever invites to join for coffee pays the full bill. In general turns are taken with payment or whoever is more senior and/or has more money.

3.- Losing face

Not losing face is the first priority for Asians, and this includes Vietnamese who will go the extra mile in order not to lose face.

For them, not losing face in front of you, but especially in front of others is crucial. Therefore many people will say yes to anything, even if they do not understand the question or even answer or give you directions even if they do not know just not to be ashamed and lose face by admitting that they do not know something, so be very aware!

This comes in many different examples, including when upsetting you, that is why when you are upset with a servant, waiter, bank assistant...losing your temper, screaming,... will take you nowhere closer to solve the problem, more likely the opposite. However I can understand that you may feel like doing just that, and I have done so a few times, considering the common lack of customer service here.

4.- Customer service (lack of)

And it is incredible the authentic lack of customer services here, which you experience on a daily basis.

Let me illustrate it with two examples. The first one yesterday when I went for lunch with a colleague to an expensive modern restaurant; I ordered rice and a pork chop. I was given the plate, the food, the fork and… and… where is the knife? Ok I ask for the knife, and I ask again, and then I notice that my chop is cold (fridge cold) so I tell the waitress. Fifteen minutes later, when my colleague is about to finish his meal, I remind the girl again about my food and the knife. She comes back with my plate, the chop is warm now, the rice is cold, no knife but they have cut my chop into pieces…

Today, after my bank login details not working for e-banking I decide to go again to my bank, as well as to complain that I have received a text message, containing my login, my password and my telephone banking password, all in the same message none of which I have requested. Thanks god for banking security. As I can foresee problems, I ask my Vietnamese assistant to come with me.

We spoke to five people in the bank, who finally come to the conclusion that I wrote my name incorrectly in the form requesting internet access: I totally agree, I don't know how to write my name, but they do (please read the chapter about losing face and not admitting a mistake), it took five people and forty minutes to reach that conclusion… does this solve my problem? No.

Then we move about me cancelling the telephone access to my account and request that never again they send me text messages with my password. "Impossible, as it is a service the bank offers, I should be happy to have it rather than cancel it."

Ok, I am not happy, what's more, I am fuming that they are so stupid to have put all security details on a text message. I cannot cancel it… when I tell them that they either cancel the telephone banking or they cancel my account they decide to give me a solution: delete the message and be assured no one will ever send you more messages. I receive no answer none of the four times I ask how they can guarantee this. And in fact they cannot, as I am sure they are just making this up to "satisfy" me, and not lose face.

Another example of the total lack of customer service, which happens so often is that you order a beer in the restaurant, they bring the bottle to your table, unopened and with no intention to open it, and I wonder, is it so damn difficult to think that most customers will not carry a bottle opener with them and that they want to drink the beer rather than contemplate the bottle, and that for that someone should open it?

Advice: drink so many beers that you don't care anymore. Seriously, deep breath, patience, and a hell of a lot more patience!

5.- Socialising with the locals

Vietnamese like to socialize, a lot, which is a nice thing. Vietnamese tend to be very open, especially in the south, and it is likely that you will be invited to join them for coffee, lunch or dinner in one of the many available places.

In cafes you drink coffee or tea, but the main reason for going there is to socialize and talk, the same that Brits go to a pub or westerns in general go to a bar with their friends.

Lunch, but especially dinner gatherings, usually with friends and colleagues, are encounters aimed to socialize and drink more than eat, however a lot of food will flow. Usually the one who invites is likely to pick the total bill, although lately western influences, especially if friends are meeting, will lead to splitting the bill, but is not so common.

Vietnamese, especially men, love drinking beer and rice wine and can be very loud. They are enjoying themselves, and if you can deal with the noise, I find it something very nice, that people can be so cheerful together.

On such an informal atmosphere expect any kind of personal questions asked to you. Sometimes they may be considered rude by you, but in general they are just curious about you or about your differences. Just some examples of this:

When I went to Hue for the first time, one of my friends took me for coffee with her old classmates who were very eager to practice English with me.

One of them asked me as a joke how many babies was I expecting (Vietnamese hardly seen men with bellies), and another of her friends, on a more serious matter, asked me if I did not have problems to seat in an airplane being so big... In western terms I am not that big or fat, ok I am not slim, but as I told the guy, most planes are designed and manufactured in either the US or Europe where a lot of people are much bigger than me, so I perfectly fit in the seats.

One of my friends, of Indian origin was with us, and was asked where he was from. When he replied England the next question was whether his father was black because his skin was much darker than mine (I am white Caucasian) and I was also coming from England... my friend felt insulted... but better not!

6.- Meals: welcome to my table???

Meals, especially family meals are a very important part of the Vietnamese culture. Consider it an honor if you are invited to someone's house for lunch or dinner, as it is a good gesture that he or she is welcoming you as a close friend.

Bring or not to bring? It is entirely up to you, but it will be considered a good gesture if you bring some small tokens of gratitude, like flowers to the wife, and candy for the children. If the person drinks, some alcohol (foreign better) is good, however you can never go wrong if you bring a fruit basket.

When you arrive to any home, take off your shoes. Vietnamese have their homes very clean, and therefore you are expected to take off your shoes when entering someone's home (or a temple) and walk barefoot.

What is more, if you go to a traditional home, and more frequent in the countryside, expect to have the meal in the floor rather than on the table.

Food is usually put in the middle of the table, and bowls and chopsticks given to each of the eaters so that they can serve themselves directly from the big plates placed in the middle of the gathering.

It is likely that people will be putting food in your bowl, as they want to make sure that you are not shy and that you eat enough; they will also insist that you eat and drink more. It is their way of showing their gratitude to you.

Tip: if you are bringing some wine to the home and you want it to be opened in the meal, bring your own corkscrew as it is unlikely they will have one. I will never forget some time ago when I brought a couple of bottles to a meal, they did not have a cork screw, and after convincing the host to stop hitting the cork with the chopstick we agreed to put a screw in the cork and use a pair of pliers to take it out; if anything, it was very funny, even when most of the wine ended up in our clothes!

7.- Collectivism

Viet Nam is now a single country, and although there are still big regional differences, especially between North and South, and Vietnamese do not deny them, which is more, they point out them at every opportunity, when it comes to facing a problem or being under attack, the collective feeling hits and they become one.

And I don't mean this from the point of view of fighting a foreign country, but even with small things, they all act like a "family".

It is very common for youngsters and no so young to "expand" they usually large family with new members by welcoming new brother and sisters and acting as one.

For example I was very surprised in my classes when I asked one of my students a question which he/she did not know, how quickly other students would whisper the answer trying to help, even under the clear threat that they would be the next to be questioned…the collective good was more important than the individual… and this happens very frequently.

This collective sense can be seen in cafes and restaurants seating, gatherings, and how close neighbors are with each other and willing to help. So if you want to be individualist you will not fit!

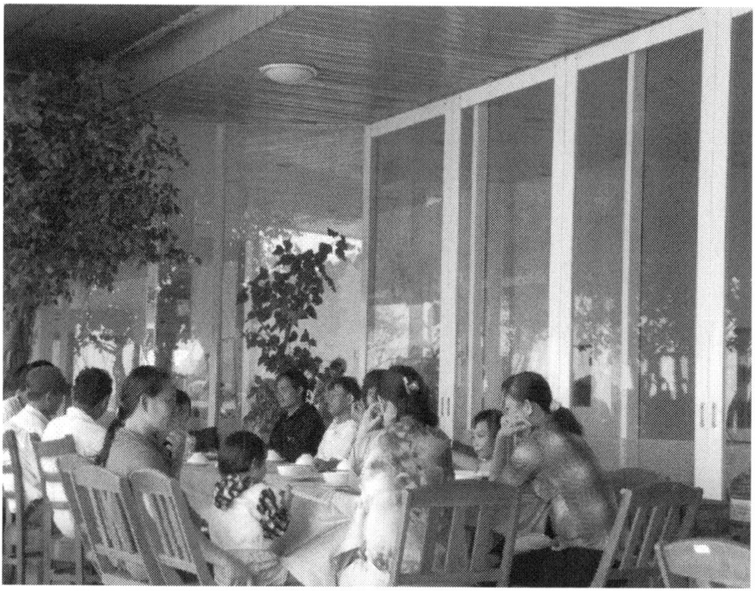

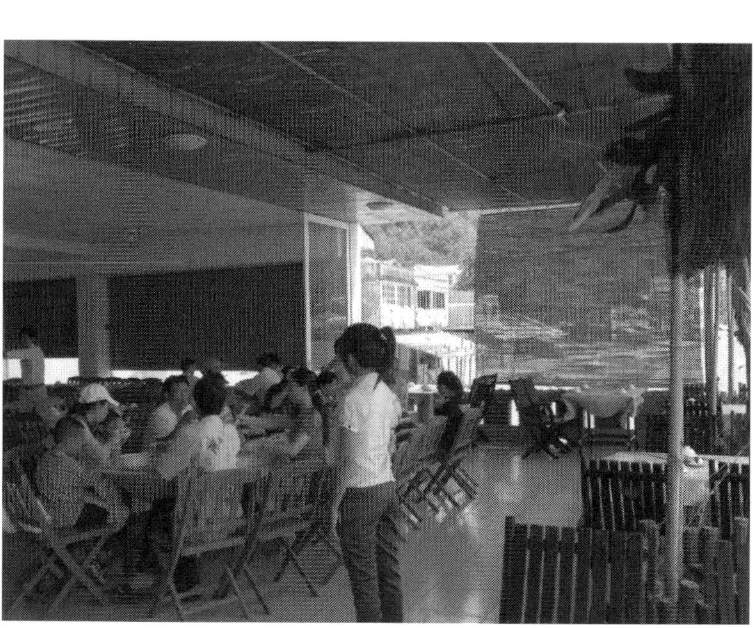

8.- Extended family

" Who is this? Oh is my older brother. But you told me you only have two sisters. Yes but is a different kind of brother"

Before you start thinking the wrong thing, have in mind that Vietnamese love to "add" virtual members to their family with whom they have absolutely no blood links.

So expect to meet people's various brothers, sisters, uncles, aunties and mothers and fathers. I have been surprised many times with this Vietnamese custom, for example I remember when a friend, whose father had died one year before, introduced me to her father... I was so confused...but you never know you maybe unsure who your father is...but when she introduced me to her two mothers...that really blew it!

Do not try to understand it, just accepted it, otherwise you will go mad.

My theory is that, linked to the strong collectivism sense amongst Vietnamese, they welcome people to their families to strength their relationship with them, being able to get closer in a non sexual way, and make a stronger group. For example hardly no Vietnamese girl will share the bed with a man who is not her partner, but if he is now a brother...

If you are really keen to know whether someone is a blood relative or not, just ask, and insist that they specify the blood link.

You can always ask something in the lines of "So is she your real sister or adopted one", it is not offensive and they will understand.

9.- I have a friend, I know someone who can help you

When you ask a Vietnamese for information about how to solve a problem, this being getting a product, a service, or whatever, they will always have a friend, relative or know someone who knows someone who can help and they will either use that connection to get what you want or they will put you in touch with them.

What they usually forget to tell you is that by doing so, in most occasions, they will get a cut of the deal.

I must say it is useful to get someone to help you get something, especially in the early days when even finding candles can be difficult, but overall expect to pay an overprice without being told so!

10.- Fast food, never be in a hurry

This is a general rule, that I will illustrate with meal times, but applies to virtually everything in Viet Nam: customer service is virtually not existent, and by being a foreigner you automatically become less desired customer for any but family run places because you don't speak the language, it is difficult to understand you,...

So if you have a meal break at work, and you want to enjoy it rather than get very upset, be very patient or go to one of the many fast food outlets or street take away places.

I usually get less than one hour for lunch, so I need to be quick. I tend to go to three different restaurants, but one is now out of the list forever as the last three times I went there, service was so bad that I refuse to go again.

The second place, I really like, portions are not small, it is more expensive than the others but most of my colleagues don't like it.

Number three, which is my favorite as food is good and portions are big, well, next time I go I may be asked to leave as today I decided to walk out before the food arrived. Justified? You tell me: I went there with my assistant, we ordered from the menu (normal dishes from the set menu just rice with beef an veggies); thirty five minutes later I reminded the waitress that we had been waiting for half hour for the food… I could not even finishing the sentence as she did not even stop walking and she said ok ok while going away…which I found rather rude and I was tempted to go after her and explain to her that when a customer talks she should listen and stop…

Fifty minutes after arriving, I convinced (well nearly forced) my assistant to stand up and leave the place. Now the waitress asked her (obviously no confrontation with me) to wait five more minutes… but that was the answer I would have expected 20 minutes ago, when it was already taking them 30 minutes to deliver. So fifty minutes wait and still no basic meal…and me being rather upset.

So we went to a different place, slightly more expensive, food was good, fast and incredibly good background music… will Vietnamese ever understand anything about customer service and why they should try to gain and keep customers? Not very soon…but those which do, will get very rich!

Understanding Vietnam Top 10

1.- Time keeping

If you are a westerner prepare to suffer when dealing with Vietnamese and their time keeping, because there is not such a thing.

It does not matter whether there is a social or work appointment, expect them to be late, and I mean very late or even not turn up at all. And do not expect any previous warning in form of phone call or message saying that they are late or not coming, and when they turn up they will usually give you no excuses and behave as if nothing has happened, and to be honest, it is better that way than getting their excuses which are just pure and obvious lies:

I will never forget, not long ago, when I went with my girlfriend to pick up her dress from the tailor for her brother's wedding even though we went to pick it up one day later after we had told it would be ready, and even though we called to confirm it was ready…when we arrived it was not ready. We were given the excuse that the trousers needed mending and had not yet been delivered, we were asked to wait ten minutes and a series of alleged phone calls were made by the tailor.

We decided to wait, while I was wondering why if she was the tailor did she sent the trousers somewhere… anyway half hour later my girlfriend chased them… another half hour later, when I was rather irritated for having to wait there more than one hour I pointed angrily to my watch… shoulders up from the tailor…

To my surprise, with no one entering or leaving the shop, the trousers materialized!

I pointed out to my girlfriend who told me that they obviously had forgotten, and in order not to lose face, they lied to us while they were making the trousers… which in my opinion was much worse, as I would have rather been told not come back in a couple of hours and use my time efficiently rather than waiting there getting my anger raising.

Of course there are exceptions to this, and many Vietnamese arrive on time.

2.- Business Meetings

Business meetings are easily unplanned, cancelled and over run without previous warning or obvious reason.

What is more, with very few exceptions, and especially if you are meeting with peers at the same level, expect them to be late, and I mean very late or even not turn up at all. And do not expect any previous warning in form of phone call or message saying that they are late or not coming, and when they turn up they will usually give you no excuses and behave as if nothing has happened, and to be honest, it is better that way than getting their excuses which are just pure and obvious lies.

It is not unusual for Vietnamese to come totally unprepared, and for example not to bring what it was agreed they would bring to the meeting. For example last week I was tasked with creating a communications and branding strategy for our company and I was put in the team with a Swiss and a Vietnamese.

To start with, the Vietnamese did not turn up at our first meeting, we both chased her, obviously no previous call or message from her to say she was coming late. We rescheduled the meeting, she appeared late, with a smile and a silly excuse. The Swiss and I click perfectly, agreed what needed to be done, who had to do it and by when, ok the Vietnamese also agreed, but she delivered nothing.

She missed the following three meeting, there was no communication at all from her (she is our Marketing and communications manager), we extended her deadline to deliver something simple three times…to end up having to do it ourselves.

Of course a list of excuses of her being busy followed, same as promises… but work or presence, no way!

3.- The ability to avoid any planning.

Vietnamese cannot plan, or actually I am sure they can, but simply they do not see the need for it. This is probably linked to their ability to simply give you the very next step for anything that needs to be done.

I have many examples both at and outside work, but one of the latest is when I asked me assistant to provide me with a class big enough for the midterm exam, which was taking place two months later.

First she gave me a funny look, and the she finally asked me what her looked meant: why do you want to know NOW, which room number you will have your exam in two months' time?

It does not really matter much my reasoning of willing to finalise the class calendar and state the class where the exam will take place, plus book the room, and in fact ensure that I will have a room big enough for the exam, her reply: "we will have to wait until the start of the term, and then I will speak to another lecturer and then we will see which rooms are available.."

I have taught budgeting and forecasting to my business and finance students, and the most difficult part was to convince them that budgeting, planning and forecasting, "in advance" was really necessary for the good management of the company.

4.- Working with the Vietnamese

Working with Vietnamese can be both very pleasant and very frustrating.

The first key is that if you want a good working relationship it is very important that you are patient and take time to know them, but especially, for them to know and trust you, because if they don't know you then you will get from them 10% if lucky!

Regardless of who employs them, Vietnamese do business, and this include work, and reporting to managers, the Vietnamese way, and for that they need to know you and trust you. This includes knowing about your personal life, you asking them about them, etc.

It is very common to have out of the office semi-formal gatherings with your colleagues, so be ready and happy to participate in them if not organize them.

When delivering work, they will also do it "the Vietnamese way":

- A deadline, is not really a deadline but something flexible.
- If you ask them to do something, they will do the very minimum step (i.e. "can you photocopy this for me", it will be photocopied but left in the copier for you to take)
- Planning is something unknown

- Being on time, is relative, so really insist on time keeping

However, they like to work hard and will always be willing to help.

Something you need to bear in mind is the high rotation, as people will move jobs if they are offered an insignificant salary rise somewhere else.

4 bis.- Negotiating with the Vietnamese

Two words: Good Luck!

And I mean it because they are very good tough negotiators. Here, with very few exceptions like pharmacies or supermarkets, you are expected to negotiate the price of everything, and Vietnamese are very good experts in negotiating, as they start doing so from very young, and they continue to do so the rest of their lives!

For example if you go to one of the local markets aim to pay between 30 to 50 per cent less of what they are asking you initially, the fact that you are a foreigner and not used to negotiate means to them that they will make more money.

If you are not reaching the price you want, a good technique is to start walking away, especially with street vendors, who will surely come after you and make you their last reduced offer, before you make yours. It is a pain, but if you get the hack of it you may get very good deals, especially with food and clothes.

On the other hand, once you realize the value of the bargain difference. Usually a few cents, is it really worth your time and the stress of the negotiation? You decide!

5.- Traffic rules

There are no rules. If you are religious, pray; even if you are not religious pray too, you will need it!

6.- Traffic rules part 2

There is a driving code in Viet Nam, that not many people knows and even fewer people follows when driving.

You will notice that hardly no one walks, and that is reflected in the lack of respect of drivers towards pedestrians, especially on peak time when motorbikes will invade the pavement and speed up and even horn so you move out of their way.

On the road Vietnamese drive as if they were the only ones on the road: going the speed they want, not using the mirrors, or looking to the sides, going to and from any road regardless of the road signals…in a few words, expect motorbikes to come from all directions at all times, at high speed.

Here when a motorbike horns is not to make you aware of a possible collision, is more like a "I am coming so get out of my way or face the consequences", as it is reflected in the many accidents that you will see, and probably have, on the roads.

As mentioned before, it is unlikely that drivers will have insurance, and I have heard many cases of collisions where the offender will simply drive away leaving the victim lying on the road.

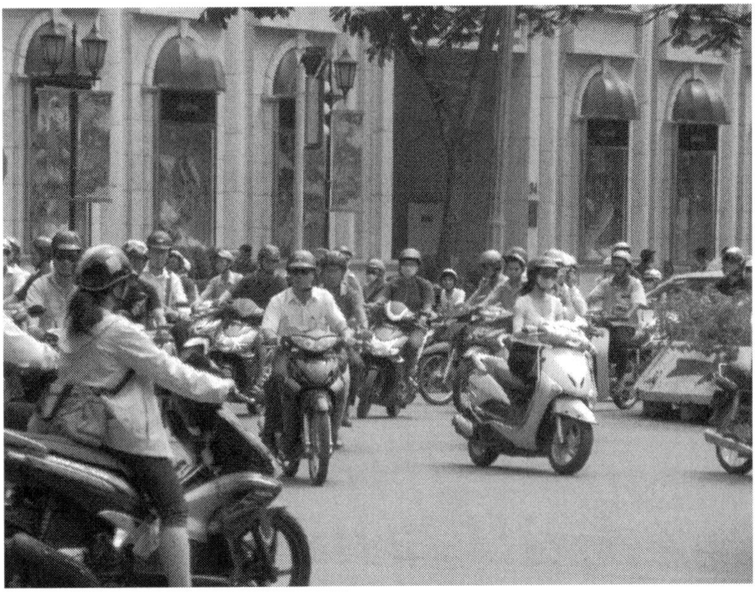

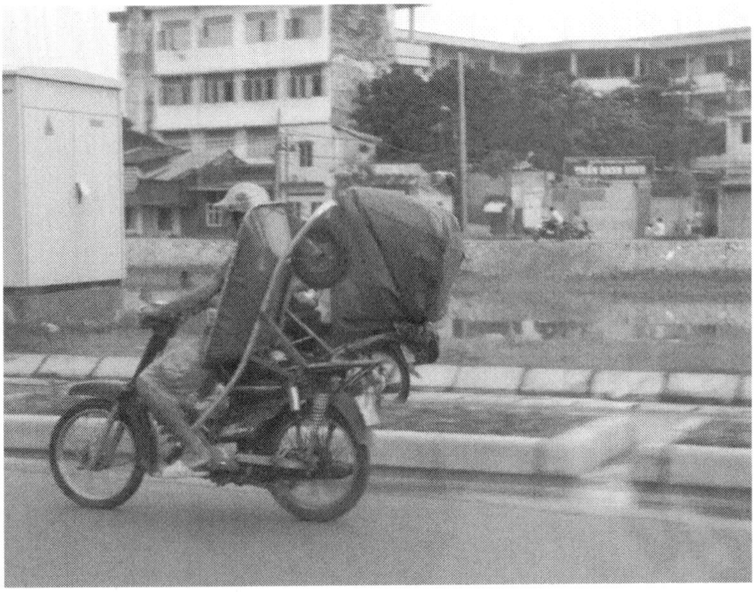

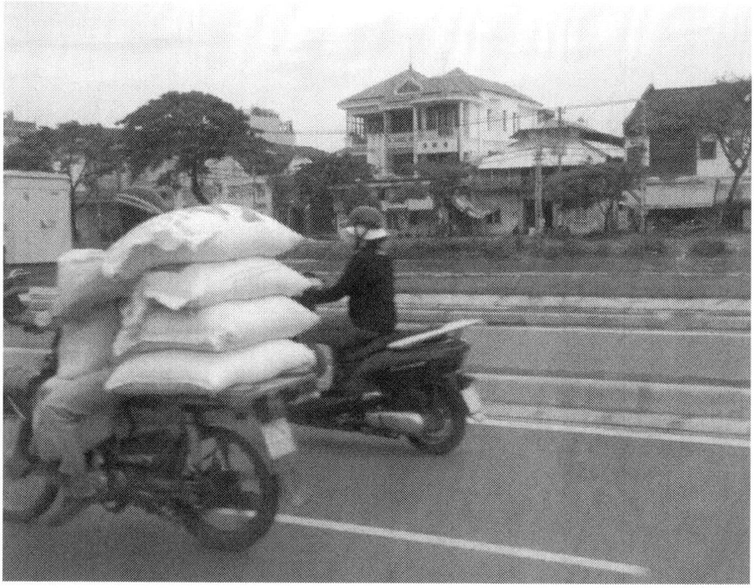

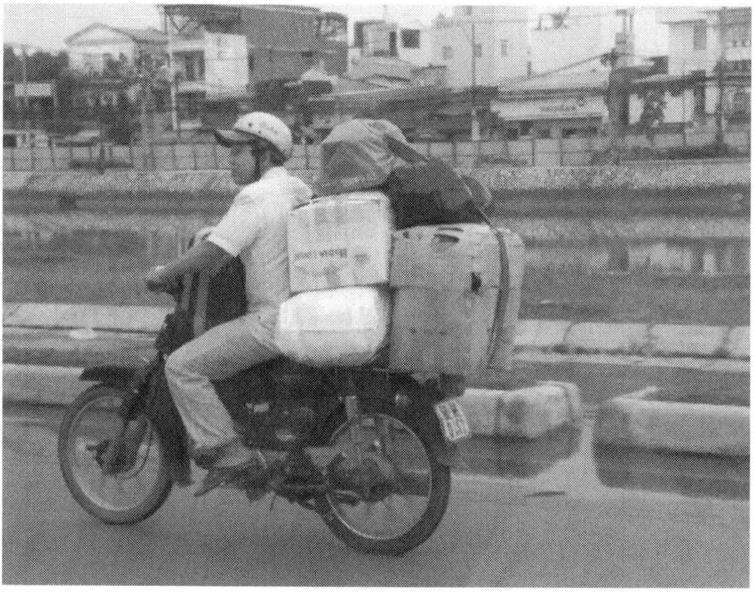

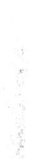

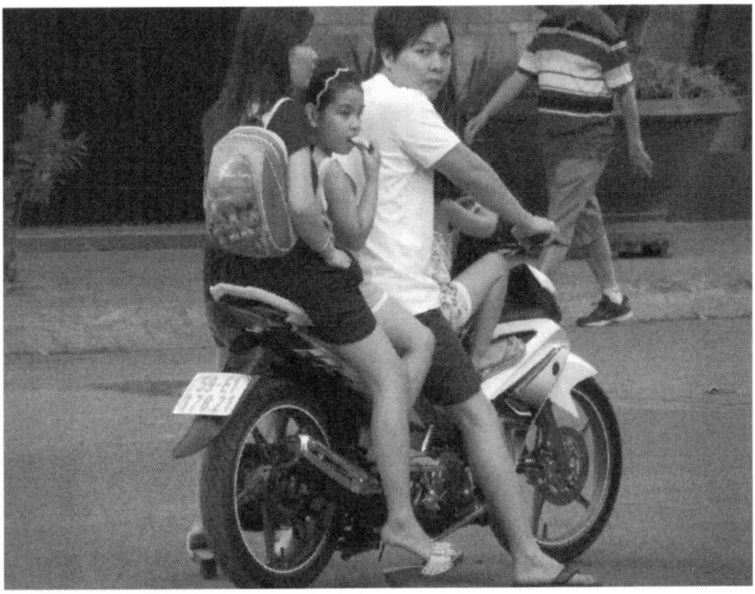

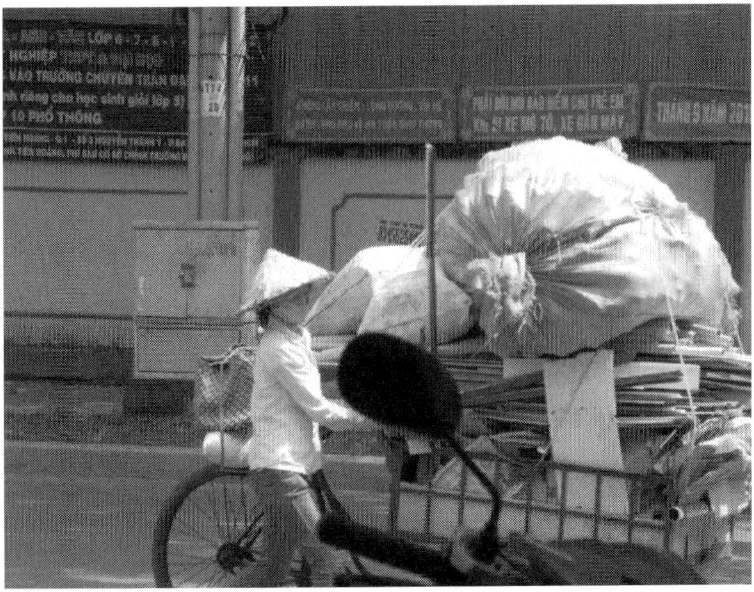

7.- Walking in Vietnam

No don't do it!

I love walking, even hiking and I have tried to do so many times in HCMC, but unless you do in the early hours of the day or late hours of the night when there is no traffic, you are really risking your life.

First you will notice that here no one walks, at least not more than from their chair to the nearby motorbike or bicycle, so the cities are not ready for pedestrians. Please don't get me wrong, major cities have pavement but full of chairs, parked motorbikes, small business carts,..and an endless number of obstacles that not only will make your walking difficult but sooner or later will make you move to the road.

Apart from the obvious dangers of motorbikes being driven in the pavement, watch out for what is coming out of the floor (cables, iron bars,...) hanging over your head, or more likely around the height of your neck (cables, ropes,...). In a few words, when you are walking you better be very awake and in full use of all your senses, or be prepared for an accident.

Also expect to be constantly annoyed by people offering you their motorbike taxi services, because as you are walking (no one walks!) they will think you are looking for a taxi. I have tried to explain to them many times that I just walk because I like walking, to what I get a mix of "are you crazy" and "you are lying to me". Lately I discovered that telling them that I walk to reduce my belly seems to be convincing enough, of course after checking my belly!

8.- Traveling by coach

Well, there are two options in Viet Nam if you want to travel long distance (here long distance means anywhere outside your city).

Several coach companies offer rather cheap, frequent trips to many routes all over Viet Nam and also to some nearby countries. Although they are generally safe, in Vietnamese terms at least, I had a couple of "interesting experiences" recently when I decided to go and spend a few days in Cambodia.

Around twenty minutes after leaving HCMC the coach made an unscheduled stop in the main road by a garage, we were asked to leave the coach and then we saw how the tires were being dismantled, moved backwards and forwards. I do not speak Vietnamese but, my interpretation is that the driver noticed something in one of the tires and decided to stop and check, being confirmed that at least one of the tires was not fine, and considering there were no spares, they decided to exchange it with one of the rear ones, both of which turned to be of no good enough quality…

Needless to say that we continued traveling to Cambodia. In the way back, when leaving the city and once the coach was full I noticed more people coming in, and being given plastic chairs, that were placed in the aisle for them to seat…nice for a 6 hour trip… not to mention the many safety implications…which at some point I decided to raise…just to get a smile back.

The other option is to secure a seat in one of the mini bus companies…there is no space for luggage, so pack light and expect to have it among your legs or on top of them. Plus expect many pick ups and drops of passengers along the trip. It is also very common for the driver to get a phone call and decide to go back to pick some more passengers even after an hour traveling…business is business…and we poor foreigners can not even complain.

Best advice: relax, take it easy, and try to enjoy the ignorance of so many things you don't know are happening! And be happy you have air con, which hopefully will be working!

9.- Complaining

I complain a lot, or so says my girlfriend, but I have my reasons. I am used to give and receive excellent customer service, therefore when I get something which is unacceptable I complain, or at least most of the time.

For example yesterday I decided to have a pizza for lunch, I should have known better…nevertheless I asked about the size before ordering, to which I was told medium, so I insisted of being told the size so the waitress drew me a virtual circle in the table, not too big but acceptable… but then the real pizza arrived…and…how could I put it…it was more like a big cookie than a pizza… definitely not the size I was told! So shouldn't complain? Well I didn't…I took a picture instead.

Complaining will not take you far in Viet Nam, unless of course you do so angrily and loudly when blame will be flying around amongst those responsible in order not to lose face. You may not get a solution to your problems or issues but sometimes you do. So if you are a quiet shy person, consider learning how to raise your voice, or suffer in silence!

10.- Children Shyness and curiosity mix

Vietnamese are very curios but very shy at the same time, especially children and women.

It is very common for me to visit places where foreigners are not usually seen and therefore attract a lot of attention, so don't be upset if people start looking at you as if you just landed from Mars or even point at you and loudly speak about you…you are novelty and you are different.

This particularly obvious amongst small children who will widely open their little eyes and will struggle to take them away from you.

Some older children may be brave enough to very briefly say hello to you as a way of bravery and curiosity; you are welcome to reply to them but they will probably smile and put their head away as they are very shy.

Sometimes I also get a similar effect from old people, while walking on the street will smile to me or say hello.

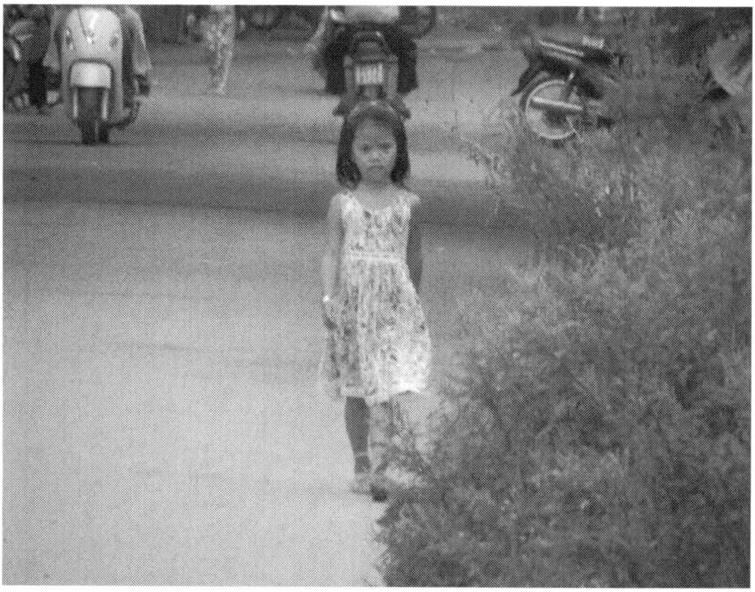

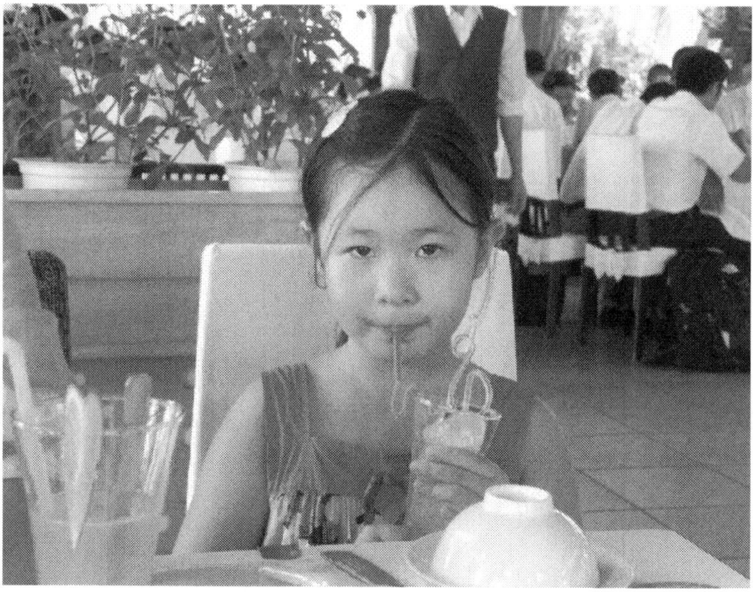

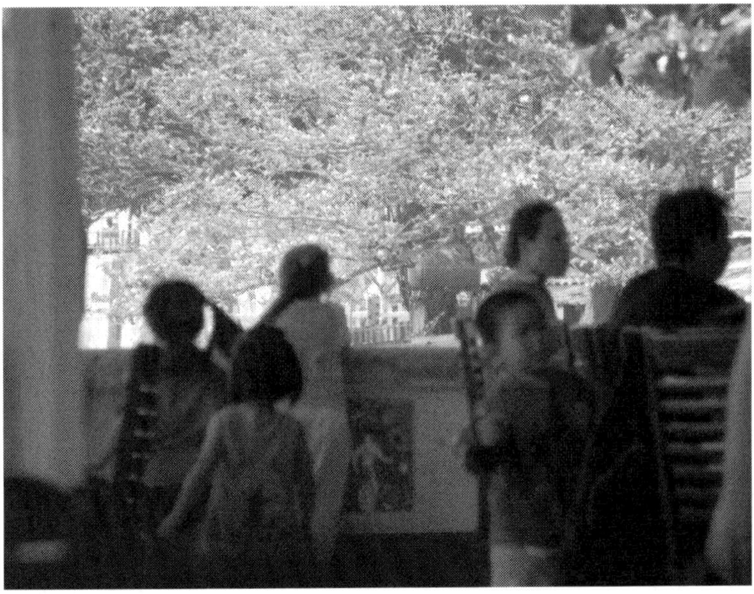

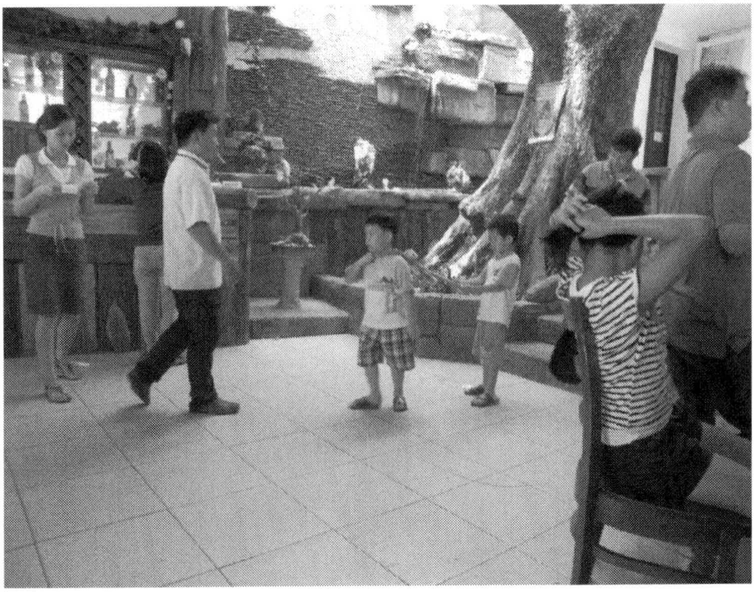

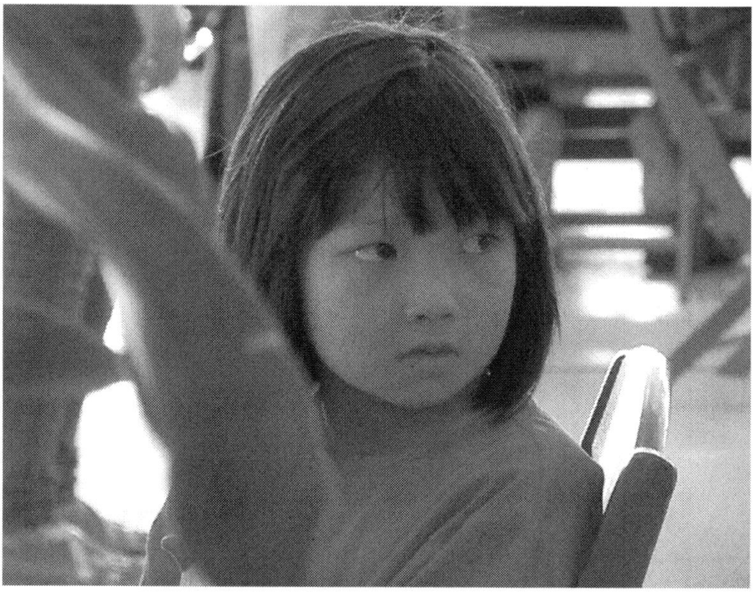

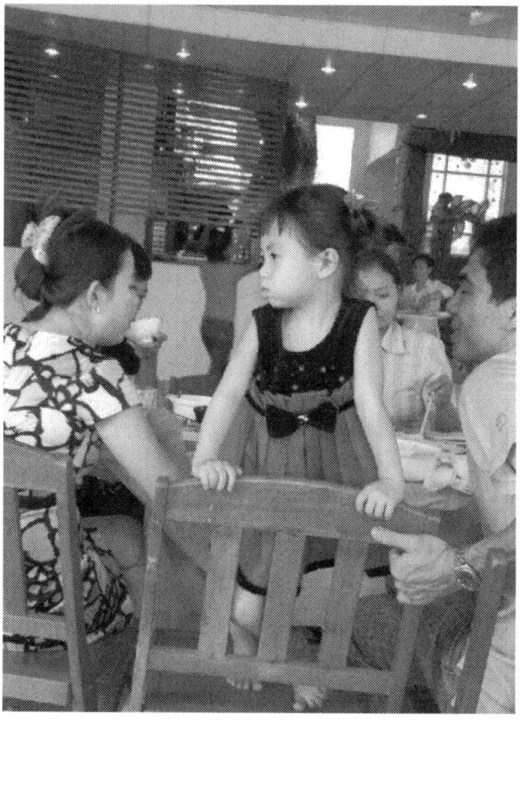

Top 10 pictures... or so

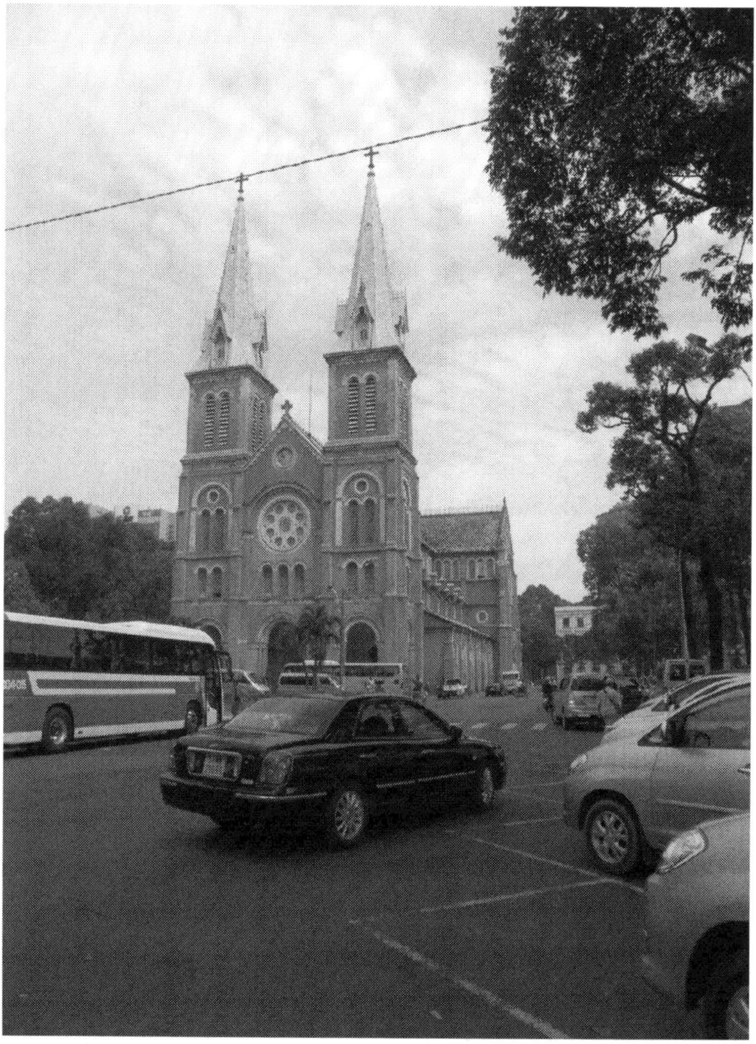

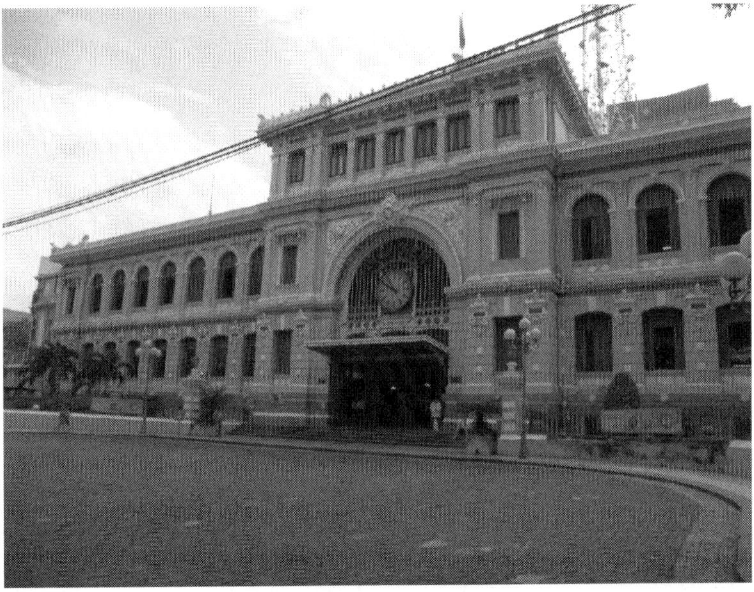

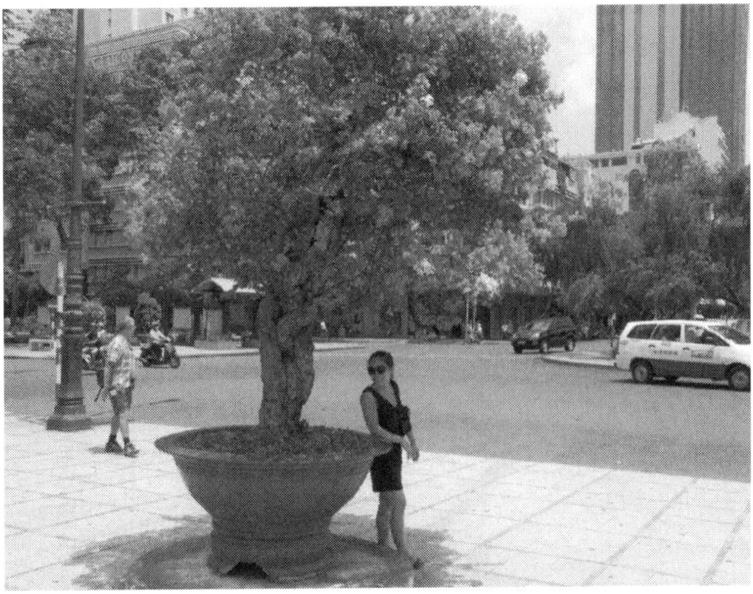

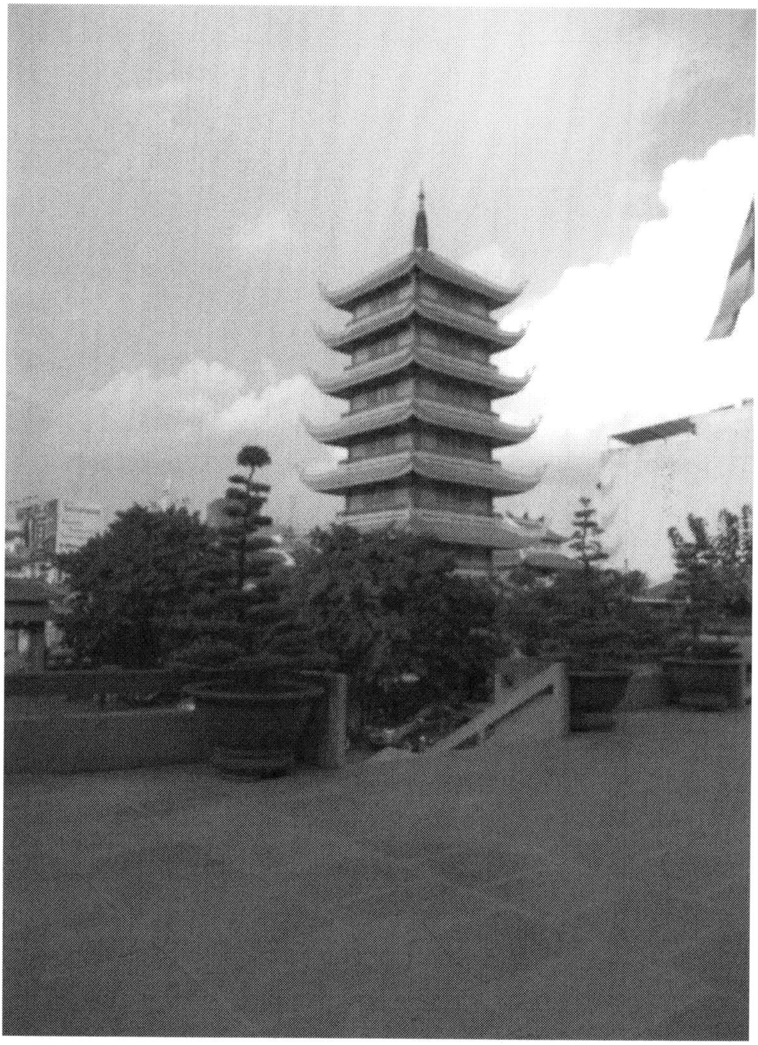

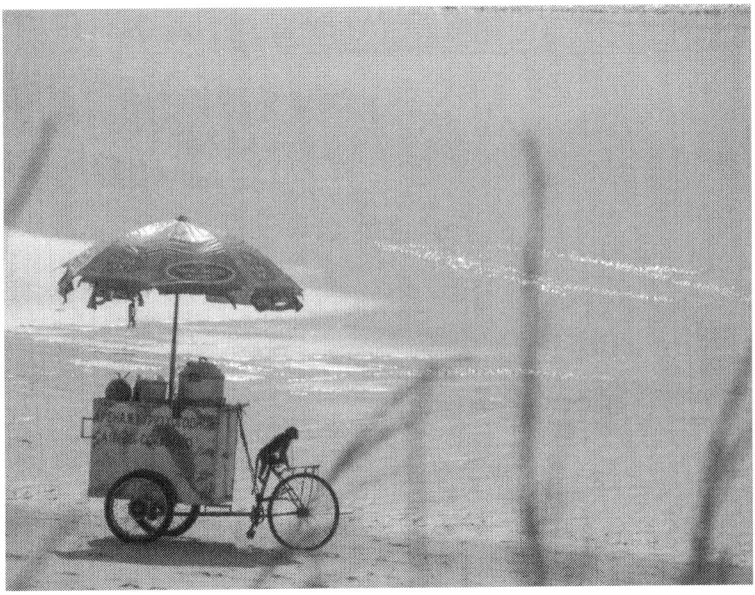

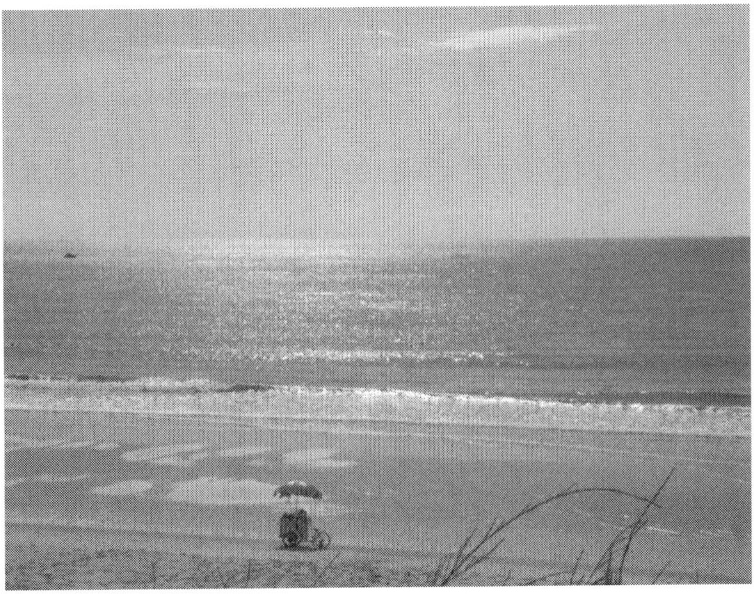

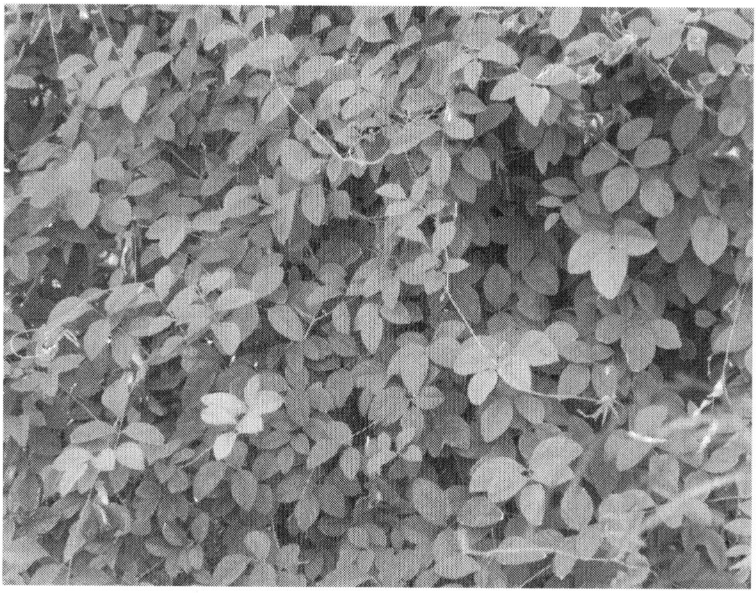

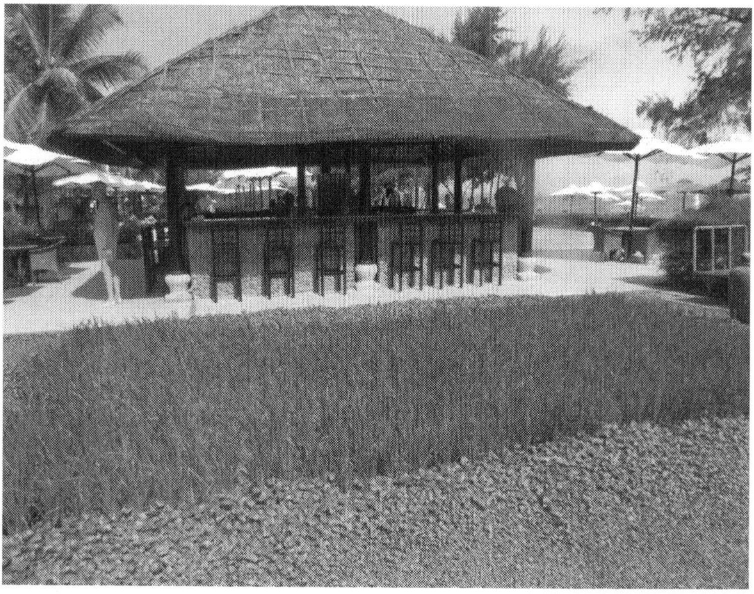

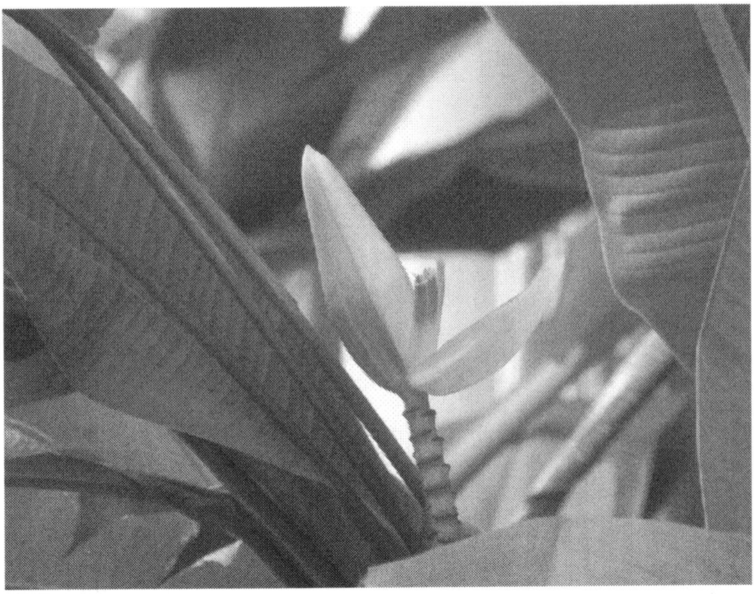

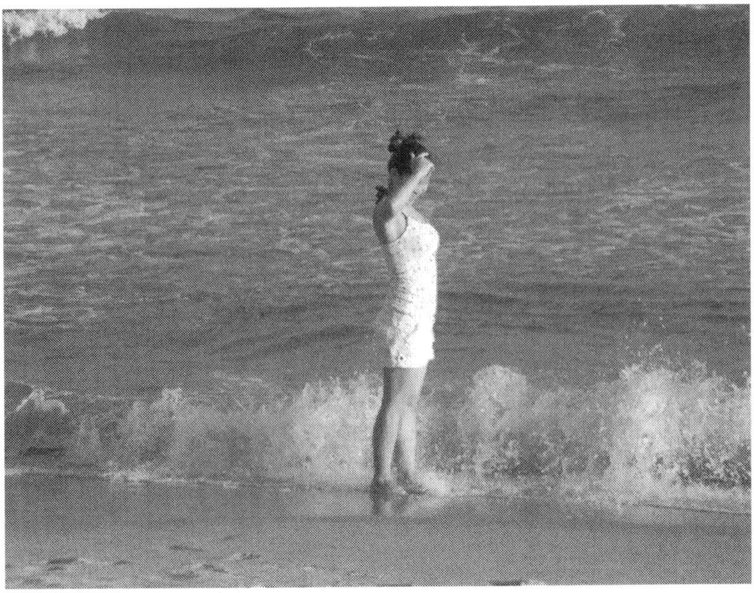

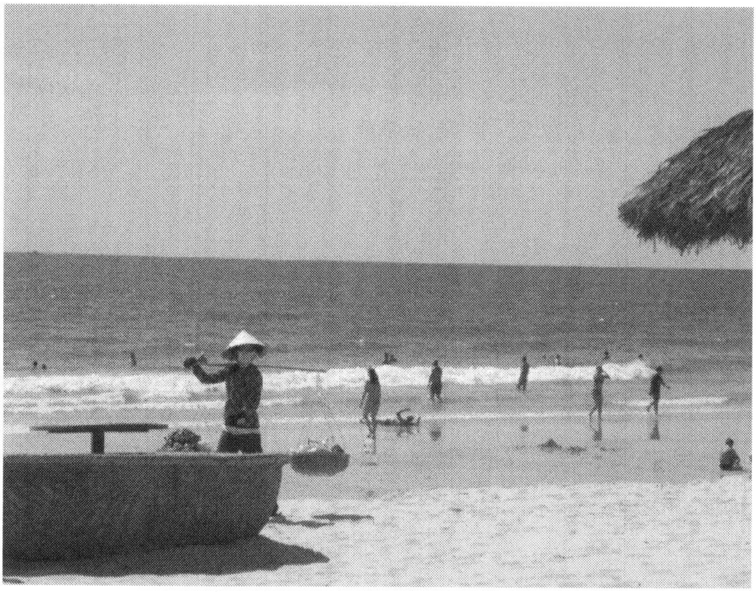

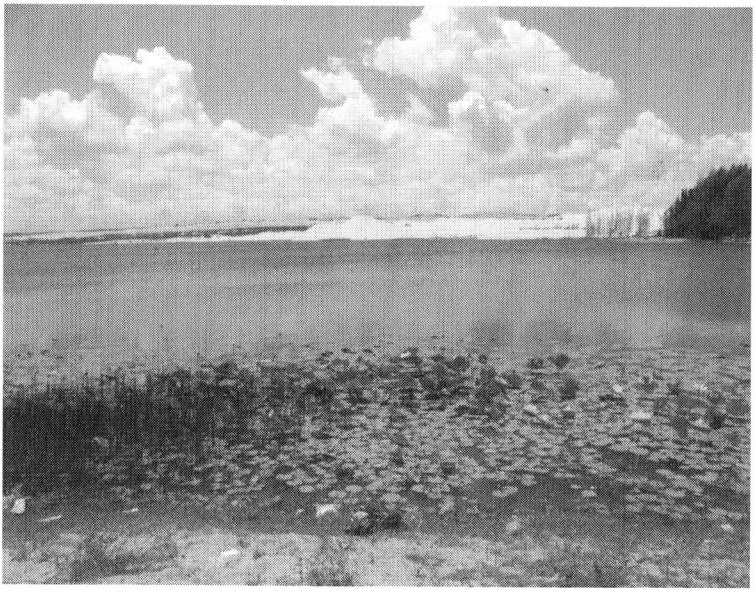

Other publications from Green Talent

All books are available from the following international retailers:

amazon.com

BARNES & NOBLE
BOOKSELLERS

Lulu

Available on the iBookstore

Vietnam Business and People: understanding cultural differences

Alfredo de la Casa

With this book, and using my experience in settling in Viet Nam, I try to help future expats or even tourists to make the most out of Viet Nam, with minimum difficulties to achieve their objectives, this being to communicate with a pharmacist or the lucky money protocol in Tet. I am also including a lot of information on cultural differences, as problems can easily be reached without knowing due to some drastic cultural differences between Vietnamese ways and Western ways. I have divided the book in small chapters so that it is easy to find various subjects. The book can be read in any order as each chapter is independent. I hope you find it helpful and enjoy reading it!

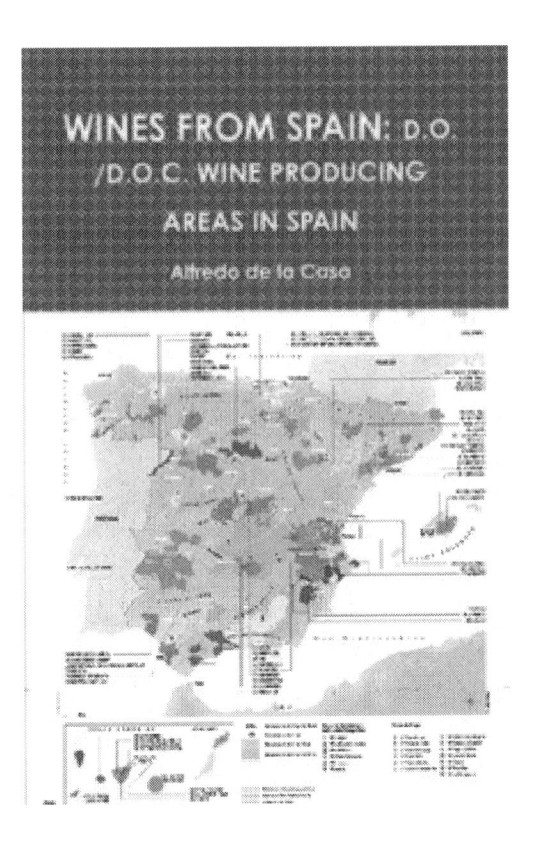

WINES FROM SPAIN: D.O. /D.O.C. WINE PRODUCING AREAS IN SPAIN

Alfredo de la Casa

A concise easy to read book with information of all the wine producing areas in Spain, including description of the various origin denominations, grapes, production surface and much more.

I could write a lot about what I think you should see and visit around Malaysia, however, an image is better than a thousand words, and here I am presenting you with over 340 pictures of beautiful Malaysia, which I am sure are better than 340.000 words, for you to see, judge and hopefully encourage you to visit Malaysia

Restaurants: How to eat well in London at low prices.

Alfredo de la Casa

In this book I am presenting my favourite 99 restaurants around London. I love eating, I love eating good food even more, and if I have to pay little for it and a good service is provided, that is what I call perfection. It is not very difficult to find a good restaurant serving good food if you are willing to pay £70 or more per person. This book is not about that type of eateries, but the opposite: after having lived for 13 years in London I have tried many restaurants, some good some not so good, here I have collated those I think you should try, with a special mention to my top 10 favourites.

Printed in Great Britain
by Amazon